Heidegger's
Confusions

"Heidegger declared Leibniz's 1714 question 'Why is there something rather than nothing?' to be the most fundamental question of metaphysics. But he psychologizes it into existential anxiety. Paul Edwards penetratingly exposes an array of Heidegger's cognate misbegotten philosophical performances."

—Adolf Grünbaum
Andrew Mellon Professor of Philosophy of Science
University of Pittsburgh

Heidegger's *Confusions*

Paul *Edwards*

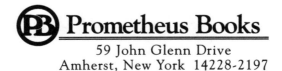

Prometheus Books
59 John Glenn Drive
Amherst, New York 14228-2197

Published 2004 by Prometheus Books

Inquiries should be addressed to
Prometheus Books
59 John Glenn Drive
Amherst, New York 14228–2197
VOICE: 716–691–0133, ext. 207
FAX: 716–564–2711
WWW.PROMETHEUSBOOKS.COM

08 07 06 05 04   5 4 3 2 1

Library of Congress Cataloging-in-Publication Data

Edwards, Paul, 1923–.
    Heidegger's confusions / Paul Edwards.
        p. cm.
    Includes bibliographical references and index.
    ISBN 1–59102–236–3 (pbk. : alk. paper)
    1. Heidegger, Martin, 1889–1976. I. Title.

B3279.H48E39 2004
193—dc22

                                                            2004013553

Printed in the United States of America on acid-free paper

To the memory of Lotte Lehmann and Elisabeth Schumann,
two great singers and two wonderful human beings

Those metaphysical philosophers are the greatest sinners, who, as if they were saying something of importance, make "Reality" or "Being" the subject of their propositions.

—Gilbert Ryle

An almost unbelievable amount of false philosophy has arisen through not realizing what "existence" means. . . . [It] rests upon the notion that existence is, so to speak, a property that you can attribute to things, and that the things that exist have the property of existence and the things that do not exist do not. That is rubbish.

—Bertrand Russell

Everything ponderous, viscous, and solemnly clumsy, all long-winded and boring types of style are developed in profuse variety among Germans.

—Friedrich Nietzsche

Contents

Contents

Preface

Bertrand Russell once referred to Kant as the greatest catastrophe in the history of philosophy. C. D. Broad commented that this position surely belonged to Hegel. Both Russell and Broad were wrong, because this title undoubtedly belongs to Martin Heidegger.

Some years ago, Anthony Quinton spoke of Heidegger's 'ponderous and rubbishy woolgathering.' Until fairly recently, Heidegger was not taken seriously by philosophers in Great Britain and the United States. Unfortunately this is no longer the case. One goal of the present study is to stem this tide of unreason.

One

Neural Kinks and the Greatest Seeker of This Century

Martin Heidegger died in 1976. At his funeral, Bernhard Welte, a Catholic priest and professor of Christian philosophy of religion at the University of Freiburg, delivered a short speech, in which he described Heidegger's 'path' as that of 'perhaps the greatest seeker of this century.' Heidegger's thought, Welte also remarked, 'has shaken the world and the century.'[1] If a philosopher's importance is measured by the number of commentaries on his work and of the translations of his books, Father Welte's remark is quite accurate. More books and articles, mostly of a devotional nature, have been written about Heidegger than about any other philosopher of the twentieth century, and his books have been translated not only into French, English, Italian, and Spanish but also Arabic, Chinese, Croatian, Czech, Japanese, Korean, Portuguese, Romanian, and several other languages. I get this information from the huge compilation *Martin Heidegger: Bibliography and Glossary*, a work of over five hundred pages which was edited by Hans-Martin Sass and published in 1982 by the Philosophy Documentation Center at Bowling Green. Sass does not list any Hebrew translations. This is perhaps just as well—the Jews have surely suffered enough already.

Father Welte is hardly a philosopher or theologian of international standing, but similarly enthusiastic tributes have been paid by numerous

---

1. 'Seeking and Finding: The Speech at Heidegger's Burial,' in *Heidegger, the Man and Thinker*, ed. T. Sheehan (Chicago: Precedent, 1981), p. 73.

influential figures. Thus, in his autobiography, Hans-Georg Gadamer described Heidegger as a 'seeker after the gold of speech and thought'[1] who 'radiated an incomparable aura'[2] and whose lectures displayed 'the brilliant energy of a revolutionary thinker.'[3] 'Why should we deny,' Gadamer asked, that 'it is an advantage to have a genius as a teacher?'[4] In a talk given in honor of Heidegger's seventy-fifth birthday and published in 1972 in his *Kleine Schriften*, Gadamer asserted that Heidegger's genius was detectable simply by looking at him. 'The very first encounter with the glance in his eyes showed me what he was,' Gadamer wrote, 'a visionary—a thinker who sees.'[5] Not only Heidegger's eyes but also his voice greatly impressed Gadamer. He noted that when, in his lectures, Heidegger reached the 'extreme frontiers of thought,' his voice, usually resonant, became peculiarly constricted in the upper register. Eventually, at the climax of wrestling with the ultimate, the tension became almost unbearable and Heidegger's voice gave out altogether. Heidegger's language made an equally deep impression on Gadamer. It seemed in fact so magical that it made Gadamer think of the occult. Heidegger's words and phrases had 'a picturesque power unequalled by any philosophical contemporaries.' They made what is mental so 'tangible' that one could not help recalling the materialization phenomena reported in the literature of the occult.[6] It might be of interest to note that Karl Löwith, who was close to Heidegger for a number of years, left us a somewhat different description. 'Heidegger could never look at anyone openly for an extended period of time,' Löwith writes. His forehead was agitated, his face veiled and his eyes downcast. If in the course of conversation, Löwith continues, 'one forced him to look at one directly, his expression became impenetrable and insecure, for candor in relations with others was denied to him.'[7]

---

1. Hans-Georg Gadamer, *Philosophical Apprenticeships* (Cambridge, MA: MIT Press, 1985), p. 52.

2. Ibid., p. 45.

3. Ibid., p. 48.

4. Ibid.

5. Hans-Georg Gadamer, *Kleine Schriften* (Tübingen: J. C. B. Mohr, 1972), p. 204.

6. Ibid.

7. Karl Löwith, *Mein Leben in Deutschland vor und nach 1933* (Stuttgart: Metzlersche, 1986), p. 43. Elizabeth King has translated this report into English as *My Life in Germany before and after 1933* (Urbana and Chicago: University of Illinois Press, 1994). Löwith's book, which was written in 1940 in his Japanese exile, is one of the most moving accounts of the degradation of German academic life before and during the Nazi years. His portrait of Heidegger is devastating.

In 1969 German television celebrated Heidegger's eightieth birthday with a number of talks in praise of his momentous achievements. One of the speakers was the well-known Catholic theologian Karl Rahner. Addressing Heidegger as his 'master,' he told the viewers that although he had many good 'schoolmasters,' he had only '*one* whom he could revere as his *teacher*.' He gratefully acknowledged that Heidegger 'taught us to be able to look in anything and everything for that *ineffable secret* which *disposes* [*verfügt*] over us.'[1] The 'ineffable secret' which 'disposes over us' is Heidegger's Being.

Unlike Rahner, the late Hannah Arendt was not a theologian and not even a believer in God. She also did not, as far as I know, believe that there is an 'ineffable secret' in anything and everything, but she gave us a similarly ecstatic evaluation of Heidegger's philosophical achievement. 'The wind that blows through Heidegger's thinking, like that which still sweeps towards us after thousands of years from the work of Plato,' she wrote in an uncharacteristically lyrical vein, 'does not spring from the century he happens to live in. It comes from the primeval, and what it leaves behind is something perfect, something which, like everything perfect (in Rilke's words), falls back to where it came from.'[2] No further information is available about this remarkable wind and its equally remarkable deposit.

Not so long ago it was almost impossible to find a champion of Heidegger among respectable Anglo-Saxon philosophers. This situation has changed in recent years. Ecstatic raptures like those of Gadamer, Rahner, or Arendt are still rare, but a number of philosophers of some prominence have hailed Heidegger as one of the great thinkers of the twentieth century. Foremost among these is undoubtedly Richard Rorty, who has been heaping praise on Heidegger's work ever since his article 'Overcoming the Tradition: Heidegger and Dewey', originally published in 1974 in the *Review of Metaphysics* and reprinted in his *Consequences of Pragmatism* (1982).[3] In his

---

1. Quoted in R. Wisser, ed., *Martin Heidegger im Gespräch* (Freiburg and Munich: K. Alber, 1970), pp. 48–49, Rahner's italics throughout.

2. Hannah Arendt, 'Martin Heidegger at Eighty,' *New York Review*, October 21, 1971; reprinted in M. Murray, ed., *Heidegger and Modern Philosophy* (New Haven, CT: Yale University Press, 1978), p. 303.

3. Rorty was one of the signatories of a letter published in the *New York Review of Books* on April 2, 1981, defending the Harper and Row translations of Heidegger's works against certain criticisms by Thomas Sheehan. The letter, which was also signed by Stanley Cavell, Hubert Dreyfus, Karsten Harries, John Haugeland, and David Hoy, expressed gratitude to the publisher and to the late Glenn Gray for making available to English readers the works of 'this immensely important and difficult philosopher.'

well-known book *Philosophy and the Mirror of Nature*, Rorty includes Heidegger, along with Hegel, Marx, Frege, Freud, and Wittgenstein, in a list of 'individual men of genius who think of something new.'[1] Earlier in the same book Heidegger is called 'one of the three most important philosophers of our century,'[2] the others being Dewey and Wittgenstein. This echoes a statement in the earlier article where these three were described as 'the richest and most original philosophers of our time.'[3] This article contains some critical remarks which are regretted in the preface of *Consequences of Pragmatism*. Rorty's view of Heidegger in the concluding pages of his earlier piece he now judges to have been 'unduly unsympathetic,'[4] and he declares it his intention to make amends in a book on Heidegger which he is 'now' writing.[5] It is most unfortunate that no such book has been published, for in it Rorty might have given some reason for his dismissal of those who do not find any great merit in Heidegger, Foucault, or Derrida as 'blimpish Know-Nothings.'[6]

Although Rorty's promised book about Heidegger has never appeared, the publication of Victor Farias's *Heidegger et le Nazisme* afforded him another opportunity for expressing himself at some length on this subject. Farias is a Chilean who studied with Heidegger and now teaches at the Free University in Berlin.[7] Farias could not find a German publisher, but a French translation of his work appeared late in 1987, and it was reviewed by Rorty in the *New Republic* of April 11, 1988. It has been customary for Heidegger's followers to excuse his support of the Nazi regime on the grounds that he was an uncritical German nationalist and that he had no grasp of practical realities.[8] Rorty has never tried to

---

1. Richard Rorty, *Philosophy and the Mirror of Nature* (Princeton, NJ: Princeton University Press, 1979), p. 264.

2. Ibid., p. 5.

3. Richard Rorty, *Consequences of Pragmatism* (Minneapolis: University of Minnesota Press, 1982), p. 51.

4. Ibid., p. ix.

5. Rorty has informed me that he is no longer planning to write a book.

6. *London Review of Books*, September 3, 1987.

7. The *New York Review of Books*, June 16, 1988, contains an excellent article by Thomas Sheehan giving the highlights of Farias's book and the similar but more careful research conducted by the German historian Hugo Otto, who has published numerous articles about Heidegger's activities during the Nazi period.

8. Typical examples of this type of apology are found in William Barrett's introduction to the section on 'Phenomenology and Existentialism,' in *Philosophy in the Twentieth Century*, ed. William Barrett and Henry D. Aiken (New York: Random House, 1962), p. 163, and in Arendt's 'Martin Heidegger at Eighty,' pp. 302–303.

excuse Heidegger's conduct along these lines, and he correctly points out that such an apology flies in the face of many facts that were common knowledge long before the recent revelations. He cannot find words strong enough to condemn Heidegger the man. He was a 'rather nasty piece of work—a coward and a liar, pretty much from first to last.' He was an 'egomaniacal, anti-Semitic redneck.' He had in fact a great deal in common with Hitler himself: 'blood-and-soil rhetoric, anti-Semitism, self-deception . . . and the desire to found a cult.'[1] None of this, however, should make the slightest difference to our judgment of Heidegger's philosophy, and Rorty reaffirms his view that Heidegger 'was as original a philosopher as we have had in this century.' We simply have to realize that, whether we like it or not, greatness in philosophy can no more be correlated with decency and kindness than greatness in mathematics or microbiology. It is 'the result of some neural kink that occurs independently of other kinks.'

---

1. Rorty exaggerates Heidegger's anti-Semitism. It is true that he did not express one word of regret about the Holocaust and that he did nothing to help any of his many Jewish students, but he did not actively harass or persecute Jews. Sheehan, *Heidegger, the Man and Thinker*, pp. 39–40, offers a judicious assessment of Heidegger's attitude toward the Jews. Löwith, *Mein Leben in Deutschland*, p. 40, absolves him on this score, pointing out that some party officials were suspicious of Heidegger because of his apparent *lack* of anti-Semitism.

Heidegger's Quest for Being

T he dominating theme of Heidegger's philosophy is his so-called
quest for Being. 'As Kierkegaard leapt from the religious stage
towards an awareness of the "holy other",' to quote Werner Marx, one of
Heidegger's most devoted followers and his successor at Freiburg, so
Heidegger leapt 'on to the shores of Being.' After the leap Heidegger
became 'imbued with a strong conviction,' shared by Marx, that 'he is the
voice and instrument of Being.' In his capacity as the hierophant of Being
he is trying to 'attain a "second beginning" for mankind.'[1] 'What is the
meaning of Being?' Heidegger himself asks at the opening of *Being and
Time* (1927), his most famous book, and two years later he concluded
Kant and the Problem of Metaphysics with the remark that 'the question
of the concept of Being' is 'the basic question of philosophy.'[2] Similarly,
in *Introduction to Metaphysics*, written in 1935 but not published until
1953, he explains his task as 'that of unfolding the truth of the essence of

---

1. Werner Marx, 'Heidegger's New Conception of Philosophy—the Second Phase of "Existentialism,"' *Social Research* (Winter 1955): 474.
2. Heidegger, *Kant and the Problem of Metaphysics*, trans. J. S. Churchill (Bloomington:
Indiana University Press, 1963), p. 255. Throughout, I quote from available English translations
where these seemed to me accurate. Where the existing translations seemed unsatisfactory or when
none exist, I supplied my own.

Being.'[1] All of Heidegger's other discussions—for example, everything he says about 'Dasein' or the nature of man in *Being and Time*—are no more than preparatory studies for the exploration of Being. The present chapter is devoted to an examination of this exploration. Such an examination will help us determine whether the claims made on behalf of Heidegger's genius as a philosopher are warranted.

The starting point of Heidegger's quest is almost invariably a set of reflections about the puzzling status of 'is-ness' or 'Being' or 'being-ness', of what we normally call 'existence'. We say that dogs and cats exist and that unicorns and centaurs do not exist, but no matter how carefully we examine dogs or cats or anything else, we can never observe existence in any of the things which exist. Although we cannot observe it, existence must be in these objects or belong to them, or else they would not exist. It should be observed that Heidegger usually reserves the word 'exists', which is obviously used in a special sense by him, for certain characteristics possessed by human beings but not by animals, plants, or inanimate objects. In his terminology the problem is to discover the meaning or nature of is-ness or Being. The question is discussed at some length in the first lecture of *Introduction to Metaphysics*, where he distinguishes two senses of the word 'being'. In the first and unproblematic sense it simply stands for a thing such as a piece of chalk or a school building. However, it also means 'that which, so to speak, "brings it about" that this thing is a being rather than a non-being—it means that which constitutes its Being, if it is.'[2] In the first sense, Heidegger emphasizes, 'being' signifies 'particular beings in respect to themselves and not their is-ness.' In the second sense the word signifies 'not individual beings, but is-ness, beingness, Being.'[3] Heidegger then formulates his 'problematic of Being' in connection with a piece of chalk. He lists its various attributes: it is greyish-white, light, and brittle, has a certain shape, and occupies a certain position. But where in the chalk is its Being? 'What then is Being in distinction to what can stand in Being or fall back into non-Being?' The same problem of course arises

---

1. Heidegger, *Introduction to Metaphysics*, trans. R. Mannheim (Garden City, NY: Doubleday, 1961), p. 81. This book, to which I will refer from now on as *IM*, contains the fullest discussion of Heidegger's 'problematic' of Being. In a short preface appearing in all editions of *Being and Time* after 1953 Heidegger specially refers his readers to *IM* for an 'elucidation of the question of Being.'
2. *IM*, p. 25.
3. Ibid.

in connection with all other things or beings: 'Over there, across the street, stands the high school building. A being. We can look over the building from all sides, we can go in and explore it from cellar to attic, and note everything we encounter in that building: corridors, staircases, schoolrooms, and their equipment. Everywhere we find beings and we find them in a very definite arrangement.'[1] At this stage the 'problematic' breaks out again: 'Where is the Being of this high school? For after all it *is*. The building *is*. If anything belongs to this being, it is its Being; yet we do not find the Being inside it.'[2]

The question recurs repeatedly in Heidegger's writings after 1935. Thus in *Kants These über das Sein* (1962) he writes, 'We say about a stone lying in front of us . . . that it *is*. The "is" here, i.e. Being, is the predicate of our judgment in which the stone is the subject. . . . What is the meaning of this "is"?'[3] In one of his last publications, *Zur Sache des Denkens* (1969, translated as *On Time and Being*), his example is the hall in which he is delivering a lecture: 'The lecture hall *is*. It *is* illuminated. We recognize the illuminated lecture hall at once . . . as something that is. But where in the whole lecture hall do we find the "is"? Nowhere among things do we find Being.'[4] We have a serious problem on our hands, and, from the outset, Heidegger is convinced that the question is of the greatest importance: 'We run (or stand) around in the world with our silly subtleties and conceits. But where in all this is Being?'[5]

In addition to *Sein* ('Being') and *das seiende* ('beings') Heidegger also occasionally uses the term '*Seiendheit*'. To Medard Boss, Heidegger suggested that '*Seiendheit*' be translated as 'beingness' (lowercase). As Boss explains it, 'beingness' refers to the characteristics which members of a class have in common, 'the particular kind of "beingness" which is common to all horses in the world.'[6] According to Boss the chapter of his *Psychoanalysis and Daseinanalysis* from which these remarks are quoted was compiled with 'Martin Heidegger's untiring help.'[7] Heidegger's

---

1. *IM*, p. 25.
2. Ibid.
3. Heidegger, *Wegmarken* (Frankfurt: Klostermann, 1967), p. 279. *Wegmarken* will from now on be abbreviated as *W*.
4. *On Time and Being*, trans. Joan Stambaugh (New York: Harper and Row, 1972), p. 2.
5. *IM*, p. 29.
6. Medard Boss, *Psychoanalysis and Daseinanalysis*, English trans. L. B. Lefebre (New York: Basic Books, 1963), p. 36.
7. Ibid., p. 49.

'problematic' and 'quest' are concerned with Being and not beingness; and it is for Being that he reserves his raptures.

Of one thing we may be sure: Being is not just another being. Is 'being', Heidegger asks in *Introduction to Metaphysics*, 'a thing like watches, houses or any being whatsoever?' The answer is in the negative. 'The Being of the building over there,' he writes, is not just '*another* thing of the *same* kind as the roof or the cellar.'[1] In *Was heisst Denken?* (1954) he inquires into the Being of mountains, houses, and trees, and he insists that 'Being is not attached to the mountain somewhere or stuck to the house, or hanging from the tree.'[2] In *Unterwegs zur Sprache* (1959) he once again asks his question: 'How does it stand with the "is"?' Is the '"is" itself another thing placed on top of things like a cap?'[3] Of course not. We can at least reach the following negative conclusion: 'We cannot immediately grasp the Being of the beings, either through the beings or in the beings—or anywhere else.'[4] There is no doubt that when we look for Being in the things around us it 'remains unfindable.' It is all very puzzling: 'All the things we have named *are* and yet—when we wish to apprehend Being, it is always as though we were reaching into the void.'[5] 'Are we not seized with vertigo,' Heidegger had written a few years earlier in *Kant and the Problem of Metaphysics*, 'when we try to determine Being or even consider it as it is in itself?'[6] Some philosophers have been tempted to conclude that 'being' is an empty word and its meaning 'an unreal vapor.' We must resist this temptation. For clearly things are and they could not be without Being. In the Postscript to 'What Is Metaphysics?' (1943), Heidegger is particularly emphatic on this point. 'Without Being,' he there writes, 'all beings would remain in Beinglessness.'[7] 'What would become of our stay in the world,' he asks in *What Is Called Thinking?* if 'this little inconspicuous "is" could not be thought, . . . if this firm and constantly affirmed "is" were denied us?'[8] The beings

---

1. *IM*, p. 73, Heidegger's italics.

2. *What Is Called Thinking?* trans. J. Glenn Gray and F. Wieck (New York: Harper and Row, 1968), pp. 225–26.

3. Heidegger, *Unterwegs zur Sprache* (Pfullingen: Neske, 1959), p. 193.

4. *IM*, p. 27.

5. *IM*, p. 29, Heidegger's italics.

6. *Kant and the Problem of Metaphysics*, p. 233.

7. *W*, p. 102.

8. *What Is Called Thinking?* p. 225.

that would remain in Beinglessness include of course all those studied in the natural sciences. Atomic scientists in particular are reminded of their dependence on Being. 'If the Being of beings were not manifest,' then 'the electrical energy of the atom would never have made its appearance.'[1] No, the words 'being' and 'is' are not empty or vaporous. Quite the opposite. We mean 'something definite' by these words, and the definiteness of 'being' is so 'definite and unique' that we must insist on its being 'more unique than all else.'[2] The uniqueness of Being is in fact colossal. 'Over against any being' there is always another being, but 'Being has no counterpart.' It is simply 'that which is most unique, whose uniqueness cannot be attained by any being whatsoever.' Its only counterpart is the Nothing, but 'perhaps even the Nothing is subject to Being and only to Being.'[3] So, far from being empty and pointless, the question 'How does it stand with Being?' is 'the worthiest of all questions.'[4]

It follows from its unique uniqueness that Being is 'wholly other' than beings and altogether *sui generis*. This makes it difficult, if not impossible, to describe Being. Since Being is a *'transcendens'* and wholly unlike beings, we cannot describe it with any of our ordinary vocabulary. For our ordinary terms have meaning only as applied to the beings which make up the world of ordinary experience. And what other terms are available to us? At times Heidegger takes the view that we can only say what Being is not and in *Vom Wesen der Wahrheit* he calls it the *Ungreifbare* (the ungraspable), the *Unbestimmbare* (the indeterminable), and *das sich verbergende Einzige* (the unique which conceals itself).[5] Heidegger always speaks of Being as 'self-disclosing' and at the same time as 'self-concealing,' i.e., as withdrawing itself from our gaze. This 'paradoxical' nature of Being seems obvious to him. When we look for Being in beings we cannot detect it there; and yet, as we saw, the fact that they *are* and are not nonentities shows that Being belongs to and is in them. In the 'Letter on Humanism' (1947), one of his most widely quoted postwar pieces, Heidegger enumerates some of the things that Being is not: 'Being—it is

---

1. *What Is Called Thinking?* p. 234.
2. *IM*, p. 66.
3. Heidegger, *Nietzsche* (Pfullingen: Neske, 1961), 2:251. An English translation in four volumes was published by Harper and Row between 1979 and 1982. The general editor of this translation is D. F. Krell, and the translators, in addition to Krell, include Joan Stambaugh and F. A. Capuzzi.
4. *IM*, p. 168.
5. *W*, pp. 88, 96.

not God and not the ground of the world. Being is more than all that exists and is yet nearer to man than all existing things, be it a rock, an animal, a work of art, a machine, an angel or God. Being is the nearest thing. But this nearness remains furthest away from man.'[1] In the end all we can say is that 'Being is It itself.' This is not an idle or trivial statement. On the contrary: 'To experience and to say this—this is what the thinking of the future will have to learn.'[2]

In his later writings Heidegger insists that we should not even say that Being *is*, because this suggests that its reality is of the same order as that of beings, and he uses the German word *west* as a more appropriate way of talking about Being. I do not know why Heidegger did not follow his usual practice of making up a verb to 'harmonize' with his noun, as in the 'World worlds', the 'Nothing nothings', the 'Presence presences', the 'thing things', the 'pitcher pitchers', and others. As things stand, translators have not felt free to say that Being beings. *West* is derived from the German *das Wesen*, which means 'essence', and at least one writer has translated *west* as 'essences'.[3] This translation has not found favor with Heidegger experts because it does not do justice to Heidegger's 'composing anew the significance of the notion *Wesen*.' These are the words of Werner Marx, who proceeds as follows: 'Heidegger began in his second phase to use this notion with new connotations, without telling his readers his radical departure from the traditional meaning of Essence. This fact has not been recognized, and has led to many misinterpretations.' What some readers have not realized is that Heidegger's new notion of *Wesen* comprises not only the 'what' of a particular phenomenon but at the same time its 'that', traditionally called its existence. Being *west* in and through the 'particular beings', and thereby it constitutes their 'what' and 'that' at the same time.[4] It should be added that not only Being but also the Nothing *west*, presumably because it is not a being and occupies a far more elevated place in Heidegger's scheme than any mere being. The same also holds for the 'Fourfold', one of Heidegger's latest 'compositions,' which will be briefly discussed in a later section.

1. *W*, p. 162.
2. Ibid.
3. T. A. Fay, *Heidegger: The Critique of Logic* (The Hague: Martinus Nijhoff, 1977), p. 52.
4. Marx, 'Heidegger's New Conception of Philosophy,' p. 472.

Heidegger refers to the distinction between Being and beings as 'the ontological difference' and he portentously declares that it 'is the *one* basic differentiation whose intensity and fundamental cleavage sustains history.'[1] The natural sciences are forever confined to one side of this cleavage, the side of beings. 'No matter where or how far scientific research extends its investigations,' we read in the Postscript to *What Is Metaphysics?* 'it will never find Being. All it ever encounters are beings because from the start its explanatory goal is restricted to the realm of beings.'[2] Modern man and philosophers ever since the pre-Socratics have failed to observe this distinction and as a result they have 'forgotten' Being. Being is in fact 'the most forgotten, so immeasurably forgotten that this forgottenness is sucked into its own vortex.'[3] 'From a metaphysical point of view,' Heidegger writes, 'we are *staggering*. We move about in all directions amid beings, and no longer know how it stands with Being. Least of all do we know that we no longer know.'[4] The situation is altogether deplorable. Five years after the complaint just quoted, Heidegger repeats that 'everybody constantly runs after beings, but hardly anybody remembers Being.'[5] What is more, when occasionally a person thinks of Being and for a brief moment considers a commitment (*Bindung*) to it, the apparent emptiness of the notion puts him off, and 'no attachment is established.'[6] I have often wondered how Heidegger knew of the existence of such people. Did they write letters to him? Or did he, in Gadamer-like fashion, look at their eyes and notice first that such a person had suddenly been dazzled by Being and then, with another glance, that he had decided against a commitment?

It should be noted that metaphysicians no less than positivists and naturalists are charged with forgetfulness of Being. In identifying their basic entity—God, the Absolute, the Will, or whatever occupies center stage in their systems—with Being, the metaphysicians commit the cardinal sin of making Being into a being. They are thus really no better than the naturalists, who identify Being with nature, or the materialists, who identify it with matter. This is a strange reading of metaphysical and

---

1. *IM*, p. 170, Heidegger's italics.
2. *W*, p. 101.
3. *Nietzsche*, 2:252.
4. *IM*, p. 169, Heidegger's italics.
5. *Nietzsche*, 2:252.
6. Ibid.

other pre-Heideggerian philosophies, but it helps to show what a lonely journey Heidegger has undertaken. Philosophers and philosophy aside, both Heidegger and his followers constantly hint that the misery of modern life is due to the forgetfulness of Being. Leroy F. Troutner, an American educational philosopher who is also a gushing Heidegger worshiper, has described the forgetfulness of Being as 'the most monumental loss in all history.'[1] It is clear that we are faced with a catastrophe of overwhelming proportions. Fortunately, not all is lost. For in the twentieth century a man by the name of Martin Heidegger appeared on the scene who devoted his life to the 'remembrance' of Being. People who 'remember' Being thereby become 'shepherds' of Being, and in this way their life acquires a new dignity. Since Heidegger's demise Being continues to be remembered by several hundred shepherds and shepherdesses in different parts of the world, but it appears that the great majority of the human race continues to be unaware of what ails it. In the words of the aforementioned American shepherd, Leroy Troutner, they are like 'sinners who do not know they have sinned before God and so do not feel the need for salvation.'[2]

THE *DA*

That man is the 'shepherd' of Being is due to (or perhaps identical with) the fact that man is the *Da* of Being. *Da* is the German word for 'here', but in the present context it has usually been translated as 'there', so that Heidegger's assertion comes to the claim that man is the 'there' of Being. The only explanations Heidegger ever offers employ such words as 'clearing', 'site', and 'openness', which are of course used metaphorically in this context. 'Within the question of Being,' he writes in *Introduction to Metaphysics*, 'man should be understood as *the* site of openness, the there.'[3] 'Man does not create Being,' in the words of the late J. Glenn Gray, one of the earliest champions of Heidegger in the United States and

1. Leroy F. Troutner, 'The Confrontation between Experimentalism and Existentialism,' in *Philosophy for a New Generation*, ed. A. K. Bierman and J. A. Gould (New York: Macmillan, 1970), p. 79.

2. Ibid.

3. *IM*, p. 171, Heidegger's italics.

the first general editor of the English-language edition of Heidegger's works, 'but he is responsible for it since, without his thinking and remembering, Being has no illumination, no voice, no word.'[1] Glenn Gray, I should observe parenthetically, was one of the more sober shepherds. He was not given to flamboyant images or ecstatic raptures, and even before later revelations he criticized Heidegger's failure to express the slightest regret over Nazi infamies.

Heidegger's teaching that man is the *Da* of Being, 'the site of openness' and 'the clearing of Being,' is supposed to constitute a great discovery. I do not see that it is anything of the kind. When the metaphors are eliminated, his assertion comes to no more than that of all known entities human beings are the only ones who are reflectively conscious of the world, who not only see, hear, touch, and taste objects but also think about them and ask questions about their meaning and value. The 'world' is here used broadly so as to include human beings themselves. Calling this a platitude is not quite right, but it hardly qualifies as a discovery. The same thought has occurred to many people, and we do not need Heidegger's obfuscating jargon to express it.

It may be of some interest to look at the formulations of this idea by two of Heidegger's most ardent devotees, who, unlike Glenn Gray, *are* given to flamboyant pictures and who have obviously persuaded themselves that we are in the presence of a great, original insight. According to Werner Marx, the shepherd whom I quoted earlier in connection with Heidegger's leap onto the shores of Being and the 'recomposition' of the notion of *Wesen*, Heidegger's teaching about the *Da* gives us a wholly new idea about the significance of human life. From the fact that the '*Da* of man is nothing but the *Da* of Being it follows that man is not only an occurrence of Being but also the open spot' and, what is more, a 'chosen spot where Being in its character and meaning comes to light.' We are confronted with a veritable 'miracle' here. For without the *Da*, 'the sense, the meaning, and the nature' of the world and also of particular phenomena could never be 'realized.'[2]

Werner Marx seems to be a somewhat innocent shepherd who does not realize that he is using highly metaphorical language which stands in need of translation. Medard Boss, an equally enthusiastic disciple, realizes that

---

1. J. Glenn Gray, 'Heidegger's "Being",' *Journal of Philosophy* (1952): 415.
2. Marx, 'Heidegger's New Conception of Philosophy,' p. 465.

he will be accused of using metaphors and flatly denies the charge. I should explain that Boss, a Swiss psychiatrist, is the creator of *Daseinanalysis*, a synthesis of certain of Heidegger's basic ideas with some of the ideas of psychoanalysis. He also seems to have been one of Heidegger's closest associates. Boss uses several of the same metaphors as the writers previously quoted, but he adds some of his own. Man, he writes, is a 'unique, primordial, luminating openness', he is a 'spiritual brightness' in whom Being 'lights up.'[1] He is 'a light which illuminates whatever particular being comes into the realm of its rays.'[2] Boss admits that this 'ontological insight' does not give the psychotherapist any new methods of treatment, but it will do something far more important for him. As a result of this insight he will gain a new and 'all-embracing' attitude towards his patients and the therapeutic process. Once the therapist 'really understands' that in man, 'as the bright sphere of Being, comparable to a glade in a forest,' all things, including of course his fellow men, 'show and reveal themselves directly and immediately in all their significance and correlations,' he will have 'an unceasing reverence for the proper value of each phenomenon he encounters.'[3] I assume that sadistic and murderous impulses and any and every kind of perversion will be among the phenomena for which the therapist will have 'unceasing reverence.' We may agree that the therapist, *qua* therapist, should not engage in moralizing, but to regard all pathological phenomena with 'unceasing reverence' is a tall order, and it is not evident that it would have any value whatsoever. It seems that when Boss tried to convert other therapists to Heidegger's ontological insight they complained that he was offering 'imaginative or poetic paraphrase without relevance for the investigations of psychologists and psychiatrists who want to deal only with real or so-called empirical facts.'[4] In reply to such contentions Boss is most emphatic that his description of man as a 'luminating brightness' is the literal truth and not merely a metaphor. It is 'a very sober and direct description of the most concrete condition of man.'[5]

---

1. Medard Boss, '"Daseinanalysis" and Psychotherapy,' in *Psychoanalysis and Existential Philosophy*, ed. H. M. Ruitenbeck (New York: Dutton, 1962), p. 84. Several paragraphs of this paper are taken over from Boss's 'Heidegger und die Ärzte,' his contribution to *Martin Heidegger zum 70. Geburtstag* (Pfullingen: Neske, 1959).

2. Boss, *Psychoanalysis and Daseinanalysis*, p. 37.

3. Boss, '"Daseinanalysis" and Psychotherapy,' p. 86.

4. Ibid.

5. Boss, *Psychoanalysis and Daseinanalysis*, p. 37.

Boss writes like a possessed man who will brook no contradiction, but it is easy to see that he is mistaken. The crucial words—'lumination', 'openness', and 'clearing'—*are* used metaphorically. It should be remembered that the lumination Boss talks about supposedly takes place not only when we see an object but just as much when we touch it or hear it or smell it and also when we do not perceive it by the senses at all but merely remember it or think or dream about it. When a blind man is aware of an object, he is just as much 'luminating' it as a man who has eyes. Thus even if one believed, ignorantly and perversely, that when we see an object it is we who are sending out rays to it and not the object that is reflecting rays to us, this would not avoid the conclusion that Boss's statements, if taken literally, are patently false. Objects are literally illuminated by rays of the sun or other light sources like lamps or candles or lit matches and not by the eyes of the perceiver and certainly not by the non-functioning eyes of the blind man or by other sense organs or, for that matter, by the thoughts and reflections of human beings.

INSIDE THE ULTIMATE

In a number of his later writings Heidegger seems prepared to offer positive descriptions of Being. He always unhesitatingly calls it 'the Open'. Being is also said to be identical with 'the Holy'. In the Postscript to 'What Is Metaphysics?' we are informed that while the thinker 'says' Being, the poet 'names' the Holy;[1] and it is clearly implied that they are referring to the same reality. Although Heidegger never identified Being with God, it has been observed quite correctly that what he says about the relation between man and Being is quite similar to what certain theologians (e.g., Karl Barth) have said about the relation between man and God. Thus we are assured that human beings cannot force their way into Being. On the contrary, if Being comes at all, it reveals itself to them by its *Zuspruch*, i.e., by 'speaking' to them. In this context Heidegger occasionally uses the theological terms *Huld* (grace) and *Gunst* (favor). It should be added that although we cannot force our way into Being, we can engage in a special kind of thinking which Heidegger opposes to the

---

1. *W*, p. 107.

representational or calculative thinking of mathematics, the natural sciences, and most philosophy. By engaging in this special kind of thinking we can greatly increase our chances that Being will approach us and allow us to stand in its midst.

In the passage quoted earlier from the 'Letter on Humanism,' Heidegger emphatically denied that Being is the ground of the world. Without explaining the reason for the reversal Heidegger did not hesitate in several of his later writings to speak of Being as the ground of *all* beings. 'Being and ground,' he writes in *Der Satz vom Grund* (1957), 'they are identical.' Nothing 'is without ground, but Being as that which grounds has no ground.'[1] A little later in the same book it is emphasized that 'only beings have and, necessarily so, a ground.' Being, 'which is itself the ground, grounds and in doing so, it lets beings be as beings.'[2] It is clear that by 'ground' Heidegger does not mean what medieval philosophers meant by *causa in fieri*. This term is usually translated as 'productive cause', and it refers to the relation typified by parent organisms and their offspring in which the cause or causes bring about the effect. Several commentators have interpreted 'ground' to mean *causa in esse*, or 'sustaining cause'. A sustaining cause need not have produced the effect, but it keeps it in existence. The air and the food which sustain living beings are part of their *causae in esse*. Numerous remarks in Heidegger's works support this reading, but in a passage in *Gelassenheit* (translated as *Discourse on Thinking*) which contains his fullest discussion of this topic, he disavows such an interpretation. He is here talking about the relations between the *Gegnet* (the Region)—the word substituted for 'Being' in this 'conversation'—and things. After remarking that 'the regioning of that-which-regions is neither a cause nor an effect of things,' Heidegger asks the question of what we are to call the relation between the Region and the things which it 'lets be.'[3] The answer is that the Region 'determines the thing, as thing,' but Heidegger emphatically adds that 'deter-

　　1. Heidegger, *Der Satz vom Grund* (Pfullingen: Neske, 1957), p. 188.
　　2. Ibid., p. 205.
　　3. In the course of a review of Ernst Tugendhat's *Traditional and Analytical Philosophy*, Richard Rorty writes in the *Journal of Philosophy* (1985): 278: 'Heidegger himself moved from the fervidly programmatic and quasi-Husserlian "fundamental ontology" of *Being and Time* to the ironic affectation of "letting go" (*Gelassenheit*) which characterizes his later work—an ironism carried further by Jacques Derrida.' Rorty has a wild imagination. There is not the slightest evidence of any such 'ironic affectation' either in *Gelassenheit* or in any of Heidegger's later works.

mining is not making and effecting.'[1] In volume 2 of *Nietzsche* we are told that it is Being which in its 'abundance' gives to all beings 'the particular mode of their Being.'[2] There is also a puzzling and much-quoted remark in the Postscript to 'What Is Metaphysics?' in which Heidegger declares that Being 'gives every being its warrant to be.'[3] Unfortunately, this is not further explained. As if all this were not puzzling enough, we occasionally get straightforward causal language which seems inconsistent with much else that Heidegger says about the relation between Being and beings. Thus in the Postscript to 'What Is Metaphysics?' in which we had been told that Being gives every being its 'warrant to be,' Heidegger also asserts that 'beings stem from Being,'[4] a statement which is echoed by Boss, who, in the chapter of *Psychoanalysis and Daseinalanysis* which was supervised by Heidegger himself, asserts that 'Being is of such immeasurable abundance that it alone is capable of releasing into its beings all that is going to be.'[5] These statements sound more like attributing to Being the role of *causa in fieri*, but in fairness it should be pointed out that they were made some years before Heidegger's conversion to the view that Being is the ground of beings.

It is clear that beings cannot exist without Being, which is their ground. Even before Heidegger came to identify Being with ground he would have unhesitatingly said the same thing, since, as we saw earlier, without Being beings would sink into beinglessness. What about the relation in the opposite direction: could Being be without beings? One would expect Heidegger to answer this question in the affirmative and prior to 1949 he did so. Thus in the Postscript to the fourth edition of 'What Is Metaphysics?' (1943) he maintains that beings can never be without Being but that Being can 'well' be without beings. In the fifth edition (1949) no more than three words of the sentence in question are changed, but they assert precisely the opposite, namely, that Being cannot be without beings any more than beings without Being. The Postscript in its later version was reprinted in 1967 in the collection *Wegmarken*. At the

---

1. Heidegger, *Discourse on Thinking*, trans. J. M. Anderson and E. H. Freund (New York: Harper and Row, 1966), pp. 76–77. This translation is frequently inaccurate. As indicated, most of the quotations are in my own translation.
2. *Nietzsche*, 2:250.
3. *W*, p. 102.
4. Ibid., p. 100.
5. Boss, *Psychoanalysis and Daseinanalysis*, p. 36.

end of this book under the heading of *Nachweise* (Sources of Publication) the following information is supplied: 'Postscript to "What is Metaphysics?" was added in 1943 to the fourth edition of the lecture. For the fifth edition the text of the Postscript was worked over in a few places.'[1] No further explanation is offered. To this day we do not know Heidegger's reason for this switch on what would seem a rather fundamental question for him.[2] In later years Heidegger stuck by the more 'this-worldly' position of the fifth-edition Postscript. In 'Zur Seinsfrage' (The Question of Being), an essay first published in 1955 and also reprinted in *Wegmarken*, '*Sein*' ('Being') is printed with lines diagonally across the word. This is meant to indicate that Being does not exist in total independence of beings.

During the last decades of his life Heidegger engaged in various exercises that would allow him (and us) a more direct access to Being. Such access is obtained by reflecting on 'the hidden meaning' in the world of technology, by analyzing a passage from Parmenides, of whom Heidegger always spoke in terms of boundless admiration, by working out the etymology of certain Greek or German words or by reflecting on what would happen if we attained a certain mood. Of these later writings perhaps the best known is *Gelassenheit*, to which I already referred. *Gelassenheit* (releasement) is the name of a special mood, and it is in effect the 'meditative' thinking which Heidegger had for many years been opposing to the 'calculative' thinking that can never rise above the world of beings. It is not a species of 'passivity,' but *Gelassenheit* presupposes 'a renunciation of willing.' To make sure that Heidegger is not misunderstood Joan Stambaugh, a leading American shepherdess, emphasizes that in *Gelassenheit* we cannot simply sit back and expect 'to drop into the lap of Being.'[3] This would indeed be too much to expect. However, no very arduous labor is required. We have to engage in a special kind of waiting. Heidegger distinguishes between ordinary waiting (which he calls

1. *W*, p. 297.

2. Karl Löwith was as far as I know the first to call attention to this flip-flop in the first edition of his *Heidegger—Denker in dürftiger Zeit* (Göttingen: Vandenhoeck and Ruprecht, 1953). In a later edition Löwith quotes and demolishes an attempt by W. Schultz, a German shepherd, to show that Heidegger's earlier and later statements are not mutually contradictory but constitute a 'dialectical unity' (1965, pp. 40–41).

3. Joan Stambaugh, 'Heidegger, Taoism and the Question of Metaphysics,' in *Heidegger and Asian Thought*, ed. G. Parkes (Honolulu: University of Hawaii Press, 1987), p. 87.

erwarten) where we are waiting *for something* and which thus involves representational thinking, and the authentic waiting (*warten*) of *Gelassenheit*, which *has no object*. In *Gelassenheit* 'we leave it open what we are waiting for.'[1] Since Being is 'the Open' we will be able to let ourselves into it if we achieve the openness of authentic waiting. We then get the following remarkable exchange:

> Teacher: In waiting we leave it open what we are waiting for.
>
> Scholar: Why?
>
> Teacher: Because waiting lets itself into the Open itself. . . .
>
> Scholar: The Open-itself is that for which alone we were waiting.
>
> Inquirer: But the Open is the Region.
>
> Teacher: Into which we are admitted by way of waiting.

. . . .

> Inquirer: I tried to get away from all representational thinking because waiting moves into the open without representational thinking. The Opening of the Open is the Region. This is why, released from all representational thinking, I tried to give myself over to the Region.[2]

Heidegger repeatedly remarks that the Region regions. By this he seems to mean that Being in some fashion comes to meet us and allows us to enter it. However, only a very highly developed form of *Gelassenheit* is the appropriate state for consummating our quest. It is only 'composed, steadfast *Gelassenheit*' which is capable of 'receiving the regioning of the Region.' Heidegger now seems to have reached a vantage point from which he possesses a clear and unobstructed view of Being. Professor John M. Anderson, the cotranslator and editor of the American edition of *Gelassenheit*, is convinced that Heidegger here 'speaks directly about Being' and 'gives an account of its nature.' He stands now 'in the midst of the ultimate' and, not surprisingly, Professor Anderson finds this an

---

1. Heidegger, *Gelassenheit* (Pfullingen: Neske, 1959), p. 44, my translation.
2. Ibid., p. 46.

'intoxicating moment'[1]—far more intoxicating I suppose than the moment when Neil Armstrong set foot on the moon. What after all is the moon, a mere being, compared with the 'ultimate', with Being, the Region of regions? What information does Heidegger relay back to earth? The following are a few samples:

> The region gathers, just as if nothing were happening, each to each and each to all into an abiding, while resting in itself. Regioning is a gathering and re-sheltering for an expanded resting in an abiding. . . . The Region is an abiding expanse which, gathering all, opens itself, so that in it openness is halted and held, letting everything merge in its own rest. . . . That-which-regions regions all, gathering everything together and letting everything return to itself, to rest in its own identity. Then that-which-regions itself is the nearness of distance, and the distance of nearness.[2]

To people who are not as easily intoxicated as Heidegger's translator, these results will not seem overwhelmingly impressive.

So far from being exceptional, passages like those in which *Gelassenheit* culminates are entirely typical of the late Heidegger. I will here quote three specimens. The first I take from an essay written in 1946 entitled 'The Anaximander Fragment' in the English translation:

> Here we think of the preserve in the sense of that gathering which clears and shelters; it suggests itself as a long-hidden fundamental trait of presencing, i.e. of Being. One day we shall learn to think of our exhausted word for truth (*Wahrheit*) in terms of the preserve; to experience truth as the preservation (*Wahrnis*) of Being; and to understand that, as presencing, Being belongs to this preservation. As protection of Being, preservation belongs to the herdsman, who has so little to do with bucolic idylls and Nature mysticism that he can be the herdsman of Being only if he continues to hold the place of nothingness. Both are the same. Man can do both only within the openness of *Da-sein*.[3]

My next passage comes from a piece entitled 'Logos' (Heraclitus, Fragment B50). It appears on the dedication page of Martin Heidegger, *Basic Writings*, a volume edited by David F. Krell, one of the most enthu-

---

1. *Discourse on Thinking*, p. 39.
2. Ibid., pp. 66, 86.
3. Heidegger, 'The Anaximander Fragment,' in *Early Greek Thinking*, trans. D. F. Krell and F. A. Capuzzi (New York: Harper and Row, 1975), p. 36.

siastic of all shepherds, who would undoubtedly qualify for the post of secretary-treasurer of the Association of Shepherds and Shepherdesses if such an organization existed: 'It is proper to every gathering that the gatherers assemble to co-ordinate their efforts to the sheltering, only when they have gathered together with that end in view do they begin to gather.'[1] I do not know what Krell expects readers to make of such a passage. He seems to proceed on the assumption that everything Heidegger says is not only entirely intelligible but so obviously true that disagreement is scarcely conceivable.[2]

My third passage deals with the 'Fourfold' (*das Geviert*)—the four 'regions of human dwelling.' These are earth and heaven, gods and mortals. Herbert Spiegelberg, not a shepherd but a sympathetic commentator, has called the 'Fourfold' a 'puzzling conception';[3] but, puzzling or not, it constantly recurs in Heidegger's later works. Spiegelberg refers to an essay called 'Das Ding' for an 'adumbration' of this notion. Here is a fairly representative sample from 'Das Ding':

> Earth and sky, divinities and mortals—being at one with one another of their own accord—belong together by way of the simpleness of the united fourfold. Each of the four mirrors in its own way the presence of the others. Each therewith reflects itself in its own way into its own, within the simpleness of the four. This mirroring does not portray a likeness. The mirroring, lightening each of the four, appropriates their own presencing into simple belonging to one another. Mirroring in this appropriating-lightening way, each of the four plays to each of the others. The appropriate mirroring sets each of the four free into its own, but it binds these free ones into the simplicity of their essential being toward one another.[4]

Passages like those just quoted are perhaps best described in the words of the unjustly forgotten Austrian philosopher Adolf Stöhr

1. Heidegger, *Basic Writings*, ed. David F. Krell (New York: Harper and Row, 1977).

2. In fairness it should be mentioned that Krell is a good translator and his 'Analysis' at the end of volume 4 of the English-language edition of *Nietzsche* shows him to be one of the less parochial shepherds. The editing of *Basic Writings*, on the other hand, can only be described as autistic: no attempt is made to break out of the obscure language of the original, and there is not the slightest awareness of objections of the kind urged in the present book.

3. Herbert Spiegelberg, *The Phenomenological Movement*, 2nd ed. (The Hague: Martinus Nijhoff, 1965), 2:747.

4. Heidegger, 'Das Ding,' in *Poetry, Language and Thought* (New York: Harper and Row, 1971), p. 179. This book is a collection of miscellaneous essays by Heidegger translated by A. Hofstadter. The original passages can be found in *Vorträge und Aufsätze* (Pfullingen: Neske, 1954), pp. 51 ff.

(1855–1921) as a form of 'glossogonous' metaphysics. Stöhr distinguished several varieties of metaphysical systems and statements. Those for which he had the lowest regard he called 'pathogonous' and 'glossogonous,' respectively. A 'pathogonous' metaphysician does not succeed in making true statements about the world. His goal is to soothe the 'suffering heart'; and, if, as theists, deists, pantheists, absolute idealists, and reincarnationists have occasionally done, he manages to bring some comfort to physically and mentally ailing human beings, what he does is not without value. A glossogonous metaphysician resembles his pathogonous colleague in not making true statements about the world, but in his case there is also no intention of bringing relief to suffering mankind. All he does is 'roll words.' Such rolling of words may not bring comfort to anybody, but, if it is done skillfully, it can nevertheless produce ecstatic raptures, as the cases of Professors Anderson, Krell, and numerous other Heidegger enthusiasts show.

WARRANTING AND LETTING BE

Statements of the kind in which Heidegger's quest culminates—'the Region gathers, just as if nothing were happening, each to each and each to all into an abiding, while resting in itself'—are not further discussable. They either say nothing at all or, if they have any content, that content remains to be spelled out. However, the earlier moves in Heidegger's quest are discussable, and there is a great deal about them that is objectionable. The main objection concerns of course Heidegger's belief that 'isness' or existence is a mysterious characteristic of things. To Heidegger this seems obvious, but it can be shown to be mistaken, and as a result Heidegger's entire quest does not get off the ground. I will discuss this issue in detail in a later section. There are also other objections which are by no means negligible. We are never told, for example, what is meant by saying that 'Being is the Open' or what evidence supports this assertion. Much the same applies to the claim that Being is 'the Holy'. Again, why do all things need one and the same 'ground' (if indeed all things need a ground) and why does the ground have to be a reality that is not a being? My dog needs food and air in order to subsist. They are essential components of his 'ground'. However, the food and the air which sustain my dog are not the same as the food and air that sustained the dog of Julius Caesar, if he had one; and they are 'ontic' or natural realities—they are beings. What is the need for Being here? Incidentally, when Heidegger speaks of Being as the ground of beings, he seems to be committing the cardinal sin of making Being into a being. These criticisms assume that Heidegger means 'sustaining cause,' and many of his statements suggest that he does.

As we saw, however, Heidegger also disavows the view that the relation between Being and beings is of a causal nature. We are repeatedly told that the relation is best described by the phrase 'letting be'; and this is taken to refer to a noncausal relation. As usual Heidegger does not offer anything that can be called an explanation, but shepherdess Joan Stambaugh addressed herself to this question in the article from which I quoted earlier. She asks us to consider the statement 'I am growing carrots and peas'. This statement, she observes, is false as it stands: there is no way on earth that she can grow carrots and peas or anything else. All she can do, Stambaugh writes, 'is *let* them grow by providing the proper conditions of water, good soil, and so on.'[1] The shepherdess is the only one among the devout who appears to have seen that, as used in this context, 'letting be' requires analysis; but her efforts must be judged to be a failure. For what she has given us *is* an example of a causal relation. The fact that the planter's actions are not the *sufficient* cause of the growth of the vegetable does not mean that they are not causally related to the end product. We have not been provided with an example of a noncausal relation that could serve as a model for a relation between Being and beings. Until this is done we must conclude either that Heidegger is committed to a causal relation, in which case our earlier objections apply, or else that no coherent position has been advanced.

As for the warranting of things by Being, the obvious question is why beings need to be warranted. Cars, refrigerators, and appliances of various kinds need warranties, but why trees and mountains? Why animals and human beings? Surely the assertion that beings require a warranter needs some justification. I am here completely ignoring the question of how one can intelligibly speak of something as strange as Being or the Region as 'warranting' something. We understand this word only in con-

---

1. Stambaugh, 'Heidegger, Taoism and the Question of Metaphysics,' p. 88.

texts in which the warranter is an observable or 'ontic' reality like a human being. What can it possibly mean when applied to the 'ungraspable,' 'indeterminate,' and 'unique which conceals itself'?

Something also needs to be said about Heidegger's flip-flop on the question of whether Being can be without beings. I will not here dwell on the surreptitious way in which it was introduced. What I wish to emphasize is that there is no way of deciding which of the two conflicting positions is correct. Suppose for the sake of illustration that Heidegger's followers were to split into a 'right-wing' faction which supports the earlier view that Being *can* be without beings, and a 'left wing,' whose members maintain that Being *cannot* be without beings. How could this dispute be resolved? Surely not by any observational tests. By 'logical' arguments or conceptual analyses? Hardly. Perhaps an appeal to *Gelassenheit* would do the trick. Clearly not. Suppose that both left- and right-wing Heideggerians achieved *Gelassenheit* and each group maintained that it confirmed its opinion. What then? It seems clear that there cannot be any reason either way and that Heidegger's option for what I have called the left-wing view is totally arbitrary and illustrates the 'anything goes' character of his philosophy. In one of his tirades against 'intellectualism' he opposes the replacement of the old calculative thinking of 'traditional logic' by 'sheer feeling,'[1] but what except emotional (or possibly political) considerations could have motivated his decision in favor of this-worldliness?

THE BEING OF THE BUILDING AND THE POSSIBLE HEART ATTACK

Let us now turn to Heidegger's starting point: his search for the is-ness or Beingness of things—the is-ness of the chalk, the school building, the lecture hall, and all the other things which make up the world. Ordinary people to whom one reads the passages in which Heidegger states his 'problematic' at once sense something very odd; and they are right. His search for the is-ness or Beingness of things is based on a false assumption, and the ordinary person vaguely realizes this. I will now show what

1. *IM*, p. 103.

this assumption is and why it is false—why, in other words, Heidegger's problematic is a pseudo-inquiry and his quest a nonstarter. In doing this I shall very largely base myself on the work of philosophers to whom Heidegger in several places contemptuously refers as practitioners of 'logistics' and whose ideas he did not understand or care to understand.

To begin with, Heidegger totally fails to distinguish between the 'is' of predication ('the sky is blue'), the 'is' of identity ('a triangle is a plane figure bounded by three straight lines'), and the 'is' of existence ('there is a God'). Thus he mistakenly believes that 'the lecture hall is illuminated' is an existential statement of the same form as 'the lecture hall is, that is, exists'. It might be pointed out in passing that while in everyday English 'is' is sometimes used to assert existence, this is not true of *ist* in German. It is only in the artificial language of some philosophers that *ist* comes to be used as an equivalent of 'exists' (*existiert*). Although serious, this confusion is not the main trouble here; the main trouble is Heidegger's totally uncritical assumption that is-ness or Being must belong to or be 'in' things. At first sight this may indeed appear to be a plausible assumption. We say, for example, that tigers are fierce, and this presupposes that tigers exist. It is not unnatural to construe this as showing that existence is a more basic characteristic than fierceness: tigers must exist in order to be fierce, but they need not be fierce in order to exist. Similar remarks would apply to other statements in which we ascribe characteristics to objects—'opera singers are vain', 'dogs are loyal', 'politicians are ambitious'. In all such statements the basic characteristic of existence is assumed before the nonbasic characteristic—vanity, loyalty, ambitiousness—can be ascribed to the various subjects.

The assumption that existence is the most basic characteristic of existing things—one which is presupposed in all their other characteristics—may at first seem plausible because of the grammatical form of existence statements. However, a little reflection shows it to be false. Existence is not the most basic trait of existing things, because it is not a characteristic at all; and it is not an ingredient or ground or source of things either. The following illustration will help us see what the word 'exists' does and does not mean. I complain to a friend that I am dissatisfied with all the secretaries I have had and that I am looking for a 'supersecretary'. I then explain that by a 'supersecretary' I mean a person whose spelling is perfect (characteristic S_1); whose typing speed is 120 words per minute (S_2); who is fluent in English, Hindustani, and Chinese (S_3); who has an expert knowledge of quantum mechanics and physical cosmology (S_4); who has a PhD in clinical psychology (S_5); and who can make excellent coffee (S_6). To this my friend replies, 'Such people do not exist.' I disagree and say, 'They may be difficult to find, but I am sure that such people do exist.' Now, clearly, when I say 'supersecretaries exist' I do *not* mean 'there are people possessing characteristics S_1–S_6 and they exist'; and when my friend says 'supersecretaries do not exist' he does *not* mean 'there are people possessing characteristics S_1–S_6 and they do not exist'. What I mean is that somebody in the world (one or more individuals) possesses characteristics S_1–S_6, i.e., that somebody is a supersecretary, and what my friend means is that not one of the entities in the world possesses all these six characteristics. The same of course applies to the statements 'cats exist' and 'dogs exist' and all the rest. When I say that cats exist I am not ascribing a characteristic to cats; I am asserting that something or some things possess the characteristics connoted by the word 'cat', that these characteristics apply to something. Similarly, when I say that unicorns do not exist I am denying that anything possesses the characteristics connoted by the word 'unicorn', i.e., that these characteristics do not (jointly) apply to anything. More generally, when we say 'x exists' we assert that the characteristics which make up the content of the concept x have application.[1] It will be convenient from now on to use less cumbersome language and speak simply of 'descriptions' or 'concepts' having application or being exemplified or instantiated.

Bertrand Russell provided an elegant formulation of the account just given, using terminology which has become familiar to students of modern logic but which is easily understood even without lengthy explanations. When we make an existential statement we are asserting that a certain propositional function results in a true proposition upon the replacement of the variable by a suitable constant. Thus 'cats exist' is equivalent to 'the propositional function "x is a cat" is true for some value of x' (e.g., my neighbor's cat Miranda). Similarly, 'unicorns do

---

1. There is an excellent concise summary of this analysis in Ernst Tugendhat, *Traditional and Analytical Philosophy* (Cambridge: Cambridge University Press, 1982), p. 300: 'To establish whether unicorns exist we do not examine the possible unicorns with regard to whether the predicate of "existence" applies to them; rather we examine the objects of the spatiotemporal world with regard to whether the predicate "unicorn" applies to some of them.'

not exist' is equivalent to 'the propositional function "x is a unicorn" is false for all values of x'.

It is evident that the grammatical form of 'cats exist' is highly misleading. It suggests that what we are talking about, our subject, is cats and that we are ascribing the characteristic of existence to them. In fact, 'cat' is the predicate and the subject is 'x' or 'something'. 'Cats exist' means 'something is a cat'. For a comprehension of this analysis it is necessary to possess a certain intellectual flexibility and to be able to look beyond grammatical appearances: we have to be able to engage in the mental 'twist' of transferring the ostensible subject ('cats') to its proper position of predicate. The intellectual aptitude required for carrying out this twist is not of a high order, but it is evident that neither Heidegger nor his disciples, who look for the is-ness in the chalk, the building, and the lecture hall, possess it. Let us return for a moment to Heidegger's example of the school building's existence. If anything belongs to the school building, Heidegger wrote, it is its existence. This is *not* so if 'belongs' is meant to indicate that the school building's existence is its most basic characteristic. The school building does indeed exist, but this does not mean that it has the characteristic of existence. It means that the thing Heidegger was talking about and looking at is a school building, or, in other words, that the description or concept 'school building' is exemplified in it.

Not only Heidegger but almost anybody coming to the subject for the first time is liable to interpret existence as a characteristic. Both cats and dogs exist: what could be more obvious than that they share the common characteristic of existence just as they share the characteristics of being animals, pets, and protective of their young! We can now see that this is quite wrong. It is true that both cats and dogs exist, but this means that both the concept 'cat' and the concept 'dog' apply to something, that these descriptions are instantiated. Using Russell's terminology it means that both of the propositional functions 'x is a cat' and 'x is a dog' yield true propositions for some value of x. Similarly, both unicorns and centaurs do not exist. This does not mean that they share the characteristic of nonexistence; it means that neither the concept 'unicorn' nor the concept 'centaur' applies to anything in the world, or, using Russell's terminology, that neither the propositional function 'x is a unicorn' nor 'x is a centaur' yields a true proposition for any value of x. As for Heidegger's assumption that existence is the most basic characteristic presupposed by all others, we can now see what real facts it misdescribes. It is quite true, to take our earlier example, that the fierceness of tigers presupposes their existence, but this does not mean that tigers must possess the basic characteristic of existence in order to possess the less basic characteristic of fierceness. It means that the predicative statement 'tigers are fierce' logically presupposes the existential statement 'tigers exist'; and the latter statement does not of course ascribe the characteristic of existence to tigers but asserts that the description 'tiger' applies to something.

It is evident that grammatical form is not a dependable guide to the meaning or content of statements. People who do not see this in connection with existential statements usually have no difficulty in grasping the point when we deal with statements whose grammatical subject is the word 'nothing'. In 'nothing is both red and blue all over' we are obviously not referring to a remarkable entity, 'the nothing', which is affirmed to be both red and blue all over. What we mean is that there is not *anything* which is both red and blue all over. Our real or 'logical' subject is 'anything' and the word 'nothing' indicates that we are *denying* of anything that it is both blue and red all over. In Russell's terminology: the propositional function 'x is red and blue all over' is false for all values of x.

Some of the clarifications of existential statements explained above are due to Kant, but, aside from some backsliding, Kant did not succeed in providing an adequate positive account of existence. He realized that the word 'exists' is not the name of a characteristic, but he did not succeed in spelling out its meaning or function. This is best explained by saying that 'existence' belongs to a class of what Russell and other pioneers of modern logic call 'logical constants'—words like 'or', 'and', 'not', 'possible', and 'all'. All these words have a clear meaning and play an important role in our language, but they are not the names of characteristics, natural or supernatural, or of things or any kind of reality, familiar or mysterious. If I say, 'At the reception I shall wear a black or a blue tie (but definitely not a red or a green one),' everybody understands this statement, although I cannot point to any thing or characteristic which is designated by 'or'. The use of the word 'or' indicates that I am engaging in the operation of disjunction rather than for example in the operation of conjunction or negation; and the fact that I cannot anywhere in the world detect 'or-ness' does not deprive the word 'or' of its meaning or usefulness. Similar remarks apply to all the other logical constants. That 'exists' is a logical constant and, more specifically, what logicians mean by a quantifier, can easily be seen when one reflects that in any existential statement we can remove the word 'exists' from the content part and insert 'there is' or 'there are' into what we might call the 'logical machinery' part without in any way changing the meaning of the original statement. 'Cats exist' can be rewritten as 'there is something, *x*, which is a cat' or more simply 'there are cats', or 'there is a cat'; and quite clearly 'there is' or 'there are' are not expressions which designate a characteristic.

As a parallel it will be instructive to consider the use of the word 'possible' in such a statement as 'the foreign secretary was admitted to the hospital with a possible heart attack'. Grammatically, 'possible' functions here as an adjective, as if it qualified 'heart attack' in the way in which 'mild' or 'serious' might do so. However, neither the most careful examination of the foreign secretary's heart nor of anything else will show us the characteristics designated by the word 'possible'. A Heideggerian might then construct a 'problematic of possibility' and argue that since a heart attack on the foreign secretary's part was certainly a possibility, it must somehow 'belong' to him or to his heart. However, since we cannot perceive this possibility it must be a *transcendens*, 'wholly other,' 'ungraspable,' 'indeterminable,' and all the rest. Human beings talk and think a great deal about specific possibilities—a possible salary raise, a possible election victory, a possible heart attack, a possible plane crash, but who among them remembers *die Möglichkeit als solche*, possibility as such, the Possibility of possibilities, the Possibleness? Human beings have forgotten the Possibleness. If one of them perchance does remember it for a moment, he is so overwhelmed by its magnificence that he at once returns to some mundane and vulgar possibility like a possible cure for cancer or a possible killing on the stock market. As a result the Possibleness is so totally and pitifully forgotten that not even the forgottenness of Being remotely compares with it in forgottenness. There is evidently a field day here for shepherds and shepherdesses to rescue the human race from disaster. The 'problematic of possibleness' as well as its mystical resolution are avoided once we see that, although, grammatically, 'possible' occupies the place of an adjective, its real function is that of a logical operator. 'The foreign secretary suffered a possible heart attack' is equivalent to 'it is possible that the foreign secretary suffered a heart attack'; and there is now clearly no need for a Heideggerian search or quest.

It should be remarked that what Heidegger says about the 'ontological difference' is *in a sense* quite true. He is right to maintain that Being is not a being, but the truth behind this is nothing more than that the word 'exists' is a logical constant and not the name of a thing or characteristic. Furthermore, the word 'exists' does have a unique function—its function as a logical constant is significantly different from that of other logical constants—but this does not mean that it designates a unique and mysterious reality. Things may well have mysterious characteristics and mysterious ingredients, mysterious sources and grounds, but existence cannot be one of them.

A few words are also in order concerning Heidegger's 'discovery' of the 'paradoxical nature of Being,' its 'mysterious tendency' to reveal as well as to conceal itself in beings—a kind of cosmic and eternal striptease. This theme is endlessly repeated in Heidegger's later works. We can now see that there is no 'mystery' at all here and that Heidegger has not discovered anything. The 'concealment' of Being is a way of referring to the fact that when we look for existence in things we cannot find it; the 'revelation' of Being is a needlessly mystical way of saying that things nevertheless exist. We may fairly characterize Heidegger's discovery of the 'paradoxical nature of Being' as a bombastic redescription of these facts; and, unlike the analysis of existential statements outlined above, it does nothing to explain them.

It may be of some interest to consider a criticism of Kant offered by William Barrett, who, unlike most other shepherds, is aware that what Kant and Russell have said about existence constitutes a grave menace to Heidegger's quest. In connection with his illustration of the concept of a hundred dollars Kant remarked that there is not one cent more or less in a hundred merely possible dollars than in a hundred real ones. Kant, according to Barrett, was also 'candid enough' to admit that unlike the merely possible hundred dollars, the real ones make a difference to his financial position. Why, asks Barrett, 'this grudging concession to the earthly fact of one's financial position, almost by way of accidental footnote?' The ordinary citizen 'knows very well the difference between a hundred merely possible dollars (of which he may dream) and a hundred real dollars.' Barrett regards this as a powerful commonsense argument against Kant's denial that existence is a characteristic. The ordinary citizen 'might be provoked . . . to exclaim that if the concepts of philosophers allow no difference between a hundred real dollars and a hundred merely possible dollars, then so much the worse for the concepts of philosophers.'[1]

This superficially plausible argument is seen to be invalid if we keep in mind what alone is the point at issue. It is whether existence is a characteristic of existing objects. Heidegger assumes this. Kant and Russell deny it. Let us suppose that A needs money to pay his rent but does not have a cent in his possession. He dreams of having a hundred dollars, which would enable him to pay his rent. This is a mere dream of possessing a hundred dollars. The afternoon after his dream a rich uncle visits A and gives him a hundred dollars. Barrett believes that the merely dreamt hundred dollars lack the characteristic of existence, which the physical hundred dollars donated by the uncle possess. This is not so. It is perfectly true that there are significant differences here. The 'real' hundred dollars have *physical* existence. They possess certain characteristics—those referred to by the words 'physical' or 'material'—which the dream dollars lack. They have mass, they occupy space, and they are publicly observable. This is why they enable A to pay the rent. There is not the slightest reason to suppose that they possess the further characteristic of existence. It should be remembered that the dream which A had existed no less than the physical hundred dollars. The word 'exists' means exactly the same when we assert the existence of the dream as it does when we assert the existence of the physical hundred dollars, although of course *what* we assert is very different. In the one case we assert that there is something which is a dream of a hundred dollars; in the other, that there is something which is an instance of a physical hundred dollars. Barrett confuses physicality with existence. They are not the same, as is evident from the fact that 'physical objects exist' is not a tautology. In Kant's terminology 'physical' *is* a real predicate, but this does not mean that 'exists' is one also. We could of course *decide* to make 'exists' mean the same as 'physical'. This would not help Heidegger's cause, and it would also lead to nothing but confusion. For we would still need a word to do the job

---

1. William Barrett, *Irrational Man* (Garden City, NY: Doubleday, 1958), p. 263.

which 'exists' now does, i.e., that of enabling us to assert that a given characteristic or set of characteristics applies to something.

Following Barrett's own suggestion I conducted this discussion in terms of the difference between the dream of a hundred dollars and its physical counterpart, but it could have been done in terms of Kant's terminology of concept and object. It is clear that Kant's 'grudging concession' about the improvement in his financial position by the physical hundred dollars but not by the corresponding concept is not in any way an admission of defeat; and it is not of course a grudging concession at all. Kant's thesis is not that objects corresponding to a given concept *are* these concepts; his thesis is that the existence of an object corresponding to a given concept is not a characteristic of the object. The concept of a hundred dollars is certainly not identical with a hundred physical dollars, but for that matter neither is the concept of a dream of a hundred dollars identical with such a dream. We can eat tomatoes and pears but not the corresponding concepts. None of this has the slightest tendency to show that the existence of any of these things—tomatoes, pears, hundred-dollar bills, or dreams of hundred-dollar bills—is one of their characteristics, which is the only point at issue.

Existentialist writers are fond of remarking that in order to 'logicize' or do any kind of philosophy a person must 'first exist.'[1] More generally, it is suggested that since 'exists' sometimes means 'alive' and since 'alive' is obviously the name of certain characteristics, existence must at least in these cases be a characteristic. This is an interesting objection, but it is invalid. We have to distinguish two very different situations in which we say that somebody or something is alive. In the first we contrast living with dead bodies or animate with inanimate objects. Let us suppose that I am an assistant roach exterminator working in the kitchen of an apartment while the chief exterminator is spreading boric acid on the floor of the living room. 'How are you doing?' he calls out, to which I reply, 'Most of the beasts are dead but a few are still alive.' Here 'alive' designates certain characteristics but here it does *not* mean 'exists'. After all, the dead roaches exist as much as those that are still alive. In the second kind of situation we do use 'alive' interchangeably with 'exists'. A conservationist concerned with the future of the mountain gorilla might say,

---

1. Barrett, *Irrational Man*, p. 271.

'Right now several hundred of these animals are still alive, but if nothing is done to stop the poachers, they will be extinct in another twenty-five years.' Instead of saying that several hundred mountain gorillas are still alive he could have said that they still exist and instead of saying that in another twenty-five years the gorillas will be extinct he could have said that they will no longer exist. A little reflection will show that here 'alive' is *not* the name of any characteristics. As asserted in *this* context, 'mountain gorillas are still alive' or, more naturally, 'mountain gorillas still exist' is entirely susceptible to the kind of analysis explained earlier. We are asserting that something is a mountain gorilla, i.e., that the description 'mountain gorilla' applies to something.

THE IMMEASURABLE FORGOTTENNESS OF BEING

If 'exists' were the name of a thing, or if it designated a characteristic or perhaps an activity, it might make sense to say that somebody has forgotten it. As we saw, however, 'exists' is a logical constant, and it does not make sense to say that one has forgotten that which a logical constant designates, because it does not designate anything. A person may conceivably forget who George Washington was, he may forget an appointment with the dentist or how to ride a bicycle; he may forget what a cruel ruler Stalin was, and he may even forget that there is such a character trait as cruelty. In the case of the putative designata of logical constants, on the other hand, there is nothing to forget. This, incidentally, is the reason why Heidegger at the outset of his quest felt that he was reaching into a void. He was looking for the referent of 'exists', and even he half realized that it has none.

There is a sense in which somebody might forget what a logical constant means, but it is not the sense required by Heidegger. A person with a serious brain lesion might forget the meaning of 'or' or 'not' and also of 'exists'. What this means is that he would no longer understand disjunctive and negative and existential statements. It is clear that this is not what Heidegger needs. The alleged forgetters of Being—mankind in general and most philosophers—are perfectly capable of making and understanding existential statements. More than that: some of them, for example, Kant, Frege, and Russell, have a very good understanding of the logical grammar of 'exists'.

There is a tendency, especially on the part of those who feel that Heidegger must mean something, to read certain things into 'forgetting' and 'remembering Being' which would give these phrases some content but which are ruled out by Heidegger's initial stipulations. Thus some readers may think of the estrangement of many city dwellers from 'nature,' and others may associate the phrase 'forgetfulness of Being' with the loss of contact with one's deeper emotions which is or is at least asserted to be very common in the modern world. Perhaps Heidegger did have some such things in mind, but he cannot mean anything like this if he is true to what he says concerning the ontological difference. 'Nature', i.e., such objects as animals and plants and forests and mountains and lakes, no less than human emotions, are beings and not Being. Moreover, if all that Heidegger meant was that modern men are estranged from nature or from their deeper feelings, this could surely have been said much more clearly without talking about the forgetfulness of Being.

Heidegger's writings, especially those after *Being and Time*, are much worse than anything the above discussion is likely to convey. In reviewing *Introduction to Metaphysics* many years ago,[1] Anthony Quinton spoke of 'its ponderous and rubbishy woolgathering,' and he observed that the book appears much better in summary than it really is. *Introduction to Metaphysics* was written in 1935, and compared to what was to follow it is a model of lucidity and concision. I have given a few samples of Heidegger word-torrents, but for the most part I have extracted the more or less discussable conclusions. No matter what the starting point of a discussion is in the later works, whether it is a passage from Parmenides, a poem by Hölderlin, or a quotation from Nietzsche, the end is always the same: Being *west*, the Presence presences, Being conceals itself but reveals itself in its very concealment or the other way around, the Appropriation appropriates (I skipped this one out of mercy for my readers), and of course the basic fact that beings are not Being. In between we get bogus Greek and German etymologies which would prove nothing even if they were not bogus and all kinds of gimmicks including the constant breaking up of German words (what Sheehan has aptly dubbed 'hyphenitis') and the coinage of new words which remain totally unexplained. As a result we are given huge masses of hideous gib-

---

1. Anthony Quinton, review of *IM*, *Philosophical Books* (1960): 11–13.

berish which must be unique in the history of philosophy. All of this is presented in an oracular style with the suggestion, sometimes made explicit, that the various pronouncements emanate from a higher power.

In his article in the *New Republic*, Rorty predicted that philosophers 'for centuries to come' will benefit from Heidegger's 'original and powerful narrative' of the history of philosophy from the Greeks to Nietzsche. I doubt this very much. What is more likely, I believe, is that Heidegger will continue to fascinate those hungry for mysticism of the anemic and purely verbal variety, the 'glossogonous metaphysics' of which his philosophy is such an outstanding example. The odds are that people afflicted in this way will exist for a long time; and if this is so, Heidegger will indeed be read and admired in future centuries. More sober and rational persons will continue to regard the whole Heidegger phenomenon as a grotesque aberration of the human mind.

Heidegger and Death

W riting in an article in celebration of Heidegger's seventieth birthday, the Japanese philosopher Hajime Tanabe speaks of Heidegger's philosophy as a 'unique and towering monument' with which the achievements of other 'contemporaries cannot even be compared.' Tanabe observes with evident delight that Heidegger's influence is 'no longer confined to Europe but reaches even as far as Japan,' and not only to Japan but to the whole world. Heidegger's disciples, we are told, 'are now active everywhere in the world.' What 'deeply moved' Tanabe in his first contact with Heidegger was the fact that 'in his thinking concern with death became the center of philosophy as well as its support.'[1] Similar expressions of admiration for Heidegger's discussions of death are found in the writings of many of his disciples. Thus, William Barrett, whom we already met, asserts that 'Heidegger's analysis of death is perhaps the most important and satisfying interpretation in his whole picture of man.'[2] Father James M. Demske, who has been deeply impressed by 'the originality of Heidegger's conception' tells us that Heidegger 'not only poses the problem [of death] with a pre-

1. Hajime Tanabe, 'Todesdialektik,' in *Martin Heidegger zum 70. Geburtstag* (Pfullingen: Neske, 1959), p. 94.
2. William Barrett, *What Is Existentialism?* (New York, 1964), p. 62. Hereafter cited as *WE*.

viously unheard-of force and sharpness' but also 'confers upon it a new ontological depth.'[1] John Wild, who does not wholly approve of Heidegger's later philosophy, remarks that *Being and Time* has 'shed much needed light' on death and that Heidegger's treatment of the subject is 'packed with suggestive interpretations.'[2]

   In the present study I wish to explain some of the reasons why I do not regard Heidegger's 'analysis' of death as a 'satisfying interpretation' and why I do not find in his discussions of the subject a 'previously unheard-of force and sharpness.' I shall examine several of Heidegger's main theses in some detail. It may be helpful to the reader if I here list the main divisions of my critical remarks:

> 1. The alleged loneliness of death
> 2. The untransferability of death
> 3. Being-towards-death
> 4. Death as our 'capital possibility'
> 5. The 'possibility' of the impossibility of existing
> 6. Living dying and dead dying.

THE ALLEGED LONELINESS OF DEATH

The first Heideggerian doctrine I wish to consider is usually expressed by the statement that all human beings die alone. Heidegger himself never uses *allein*, which is the German word for 'alone', but he uses various expressions that come to the same thing. He constantly speaks of death as a 'non-relational possibility.' When death 'is the issue,' he writes, 'all Being-alongside the things with which we concern ourselves, and all

---

1. James M. Demske, *Being, Man and Death* (Lexington: University Press of Kentucky, 1970), pp. 2, 5. Hereafter cited as *BMD*. Demske's book is one of two volumes entirely devoted to Heidegger's views of death. The other is Adolf Sternberger's *Der verstandene Tod* (Leipzig, 1934). Sternberger treats Heidegger with respect, but he does offer a few critical comments. Demske's book is pure panegyric. Like the great majority of what passes as Heidegger commentary, his book largely consists of quotations and paraphrases of Heidegger's remarks, accompanied by ecstatic endorsements.

2. John Wild, "An English Version of Martin Heidegger's *Being and Time*," *Review of Metaphysics* (1962): 305, 308.

Being-with-Others, will fail us.'[1] When Dasein (a human being) stands before its death, i.e., when he is face to face with 'the possibility of no-longer-being-able-to-be-there,' then 'all its relations to any other Dasein have been undone' (*BT*, p. 294). 'The non-relational character of death, as understood in anticipation, individualizes Dasein down to itself' (*BT*, p. 308). In this 'distinct possibility of its own self,' a possibility 'in which its very Being is the issue,' Dasein 'has been wrenched away from the "they" [other people]' (*BT*, p. 307). Death 'must be taken over by Dasein alone.'[2]

Heideggerians writing in English have used words like 'alone' and 'isolated' to express this doctrine; and in doing so, they have, I think, been quite faithful to Heidegger's intentions. Death, according to John Macquarrie, 'isolates the individual. He must die himself alone.'[3] 'This thing at least,' writes John Wild, speaking of death, 'I must do alone,'[4] and a little later he remarks that death 'is an actual act lived through by an individual alone.'[5] 'Everyone,' in the words of Calvin O. Schrag, 'must die alone.'[6] 'The more resolutely we advance toward' death, in the words of Father Demske, 'the more clearly we see the aspects of aloneness which characterize Dasein in its being-unto-death. Advancing reveals that all being-with the other beings . . . fades away in the sight of death.'[7] 'Each of us,' writes Father Ladislaus Boros, a Hungarian admirer of Heidegger, 'must accept death absolutely alone.'[8] Heidegger's analysis of 'Dasein's

---

1. Heidegger, *Being and Time*, English trans. John Macquarrie and Edward Robinson (London: SCM Press, 1962), p. 308. My quotations are for the most part from this translation, hereafter cited as M-R. Although M-R is in many ways an admirable job, on some occasions the translators, in trying to be idiomatic and avoid excessive literalness, do not give the reader an adequate idea of Heidegger's evident intentions. In such cases I have provided my own translation. Whenever I depart, to any extent, from M-R I give page references to the original German text prefaced by 'G' as well as the corresponding page in M-R. *Being and Time* is hereafter cited as *BT*.

2. *BT*, p. 308. Heidegger's original is 'einzig von ihm selbst her . . . übernehmen,' which means 'taken over by [Dasein] itself exclusively.' The M-R translation is idiomatically quite correct in using 'alone'.

3. John Macquarrie, *An Existentialist Theology* (London: SCM Press, 1955), p. 118. Hereafter cited as *ET*.

4. John Wild, *The Challenge of Existentialism* (Bloomington: Indiana University Press, 1959), p. 82. Hereafter cited as *CE*.

5. Ibid., p. 108.

6. Calvin O. Schrag, *Existence and Freedom* (Evanston, IL: Northwestern University Press, 1961), p. 108. Hereafter cited as *EF*.

7. *BMD*, p. 32.

8. Ladislaus Boros, *The Moment of Truth* (London, 1965), p. 1. Hereafter cited as *MT*.

existentiality,' according to Michael Gelven, the author of a rhapsody entitled *A Commentary on Heidegger's "Being and Time"*, 'shows us that . . . I alone will die my death.' Furthermore, 'when my consciousness becomes aware of death, it projects before me that I am really going to die, and that when I do I will die alone.'[1] Death, to quote J. Glenn Gray, 'is unshareable, the most isolated, separate of life's possibilities, and for that reason the most significant.'[2] To this Gray adds, speaking no doubt from extensive personal experience, 'I always die alone.'[3] Father William J. Richardson, the author of an enormously detailed study of all phases of Heidegger's philosophy which is widely regarded as the standard commentary on the subject, wholeheartedly accepts Heidegger's view about the inevitable aloneness of the dying individual. A human being 'dies . . . by its self [*sic*] stripped of all relationship to others, isolated completely.'[4] There is apparently something superficially very plausible about the contention that everybody must die alone. For it is endorsed by philosophers who are critical of Heidegger in other contexts, and it is also asserted, as if it were something self-evident, by people who probably never heard of Heidegger. Thus Marjorie Grene, in an otherwise highly critical study of Heidegger, is full of praise for him on this particular issue, remarking: 'It is in the face of death that each man stands most strikingly and irrevocably alone.'[5] Similarly, Leonard Bernstein, who fancied himself a philosopher and not only a musician, observed a few years ago, in a funeral oration for the distinguished mezzo-soprano Jennie Tourel, that 'she knew that birth and death are lonely acts, painfully private and incapable of being shared.'[6]

The question we shall ask about this doctrine is not simply 'is it true?' For any statement can be made true by suitable definitions. The question we have to ask is whether the doctrine is true in a sense in which it would constitute a discovery or a significant insight. Before we try to answer this question it should be emphasized that Heidegger and his followers are

---

1. Michael Gelven, *A Commentary on Heidegger's "Being and Time"* (New York: Harper and Row, 1970), pp. 150–51. Hereafter cited as *CBT*.

2. J. Glenn Gray, "The Problem of Death in Modern Philosophy," in *The Modern Vision of Death*, ed. N. A. Scott Jr. (Richmond, VA: John Knox Press, 1967), p. 55. Hereafter cited as PD.

3. Ibid., p. 56.

4. William J. Richardson, *Heidegger: Through Phenomenology to Thought*, 2nd ed., with a preface by Heidegger (The Hague: Martinus Nijholf, 1967), p. 76.

5. Marjorie Grene, *Heidegger* (London, 1957), p. 45.

6. Leonard Bernstein, *New York Times*, December 9, 1973.

offering us a proposition that is universal and, in some important sense, necessary. They are not merely asserting, what nobody would dispute, that some or many human beings die alone. They assert that this is true of all human beings in all ages and that it is necessarily true of all human beings simply as a consequence of their mortality.

I will begin my critical observations by pointing out that the statement 'all human beings die alone' can be understood in three reasonably straightforward senses and that in each of these it is quite certainly false. In a very obvious sense a person dies alone if no other human being is with him when he dies. A man driving by himself who has a fatal heart attack would be dying alone in this sense. A few years ago, Bishop James Pike and his wife got lost in the desert in Israel. The bishop stayed with the jeep that had broken down, while his wife went for help. He died before the rescuers arrived. He too died alone in the sense under discussion. In this sense many people die alone and many do not.

There is another sense in which it would be natural to speak of somebody as dying alone or in isolation, even if other human beings are physically with him during his last moments. In this sense a person is dying alone if he is psychologically isolated, i.e., if there are no other human beings near him with whom he has any strong emotional bonds. Elisabeth Kübler-Ross and other psychologists have movingly described the sufferings of dying patients who, in addition to their physical torment, suffer extreme loneliness as a result of the coldness of nurses and doctors and the inability of relatives to be open and honest. It is important to emphasize that, while a great many people do die alone in the second sense, not all do; and it is certainly not necessary, either in the sense of logical or in the sense of factual necessity, that human beings should do so.

That it is not at all necessary is illustrated in Gerhardt Hauptmann's play *Vor Sonnenuntergang*, which deals with the last year in the life of Matthias Clausen, an elderly and extremely wealthy industrialist. Clausen is a widower with two married daughters from whom he is estranged, and he feels totally alone. He plans to kill himself but is talked out of suicide by a lovely young typist. They fall in love. He proposes marriage, but she refuses since it might be thought she was marrying him for his money. They live together and eventually do get married. His daughters and their husbands institute proceedings to have Matthias declared mentally incompetent. He fights back and suffers a heart attack. As he is dying he tells his grief-stricken young wife that there is nothing to regret. 'The last year, since I have known you, is the only time I really lived—the only time that I was close to another human being.' Matthias Clausen did *not* die alone in the emotional or psychological sense; and surely the same has been true of *some* human beings in real life. David Hume, to give just one famous example, was never more contented than during the last six months of his life, when he knew that he was dying. He never felt closer to his friends than during this period, and he continued to take an active interest in the world around him, including the latest publications in various fields. 'Were I to name a period of my life which I should most choose to pass over again,' he wrote in his short autobiography while he was dying, 'I might be tempted to point to this later period.'[1]

There is a further sense in which people are sometimes said to die alone, where 'dying alone' is opposed to 'dying together' rather than to 'dying not alone'. In *The Savage God*, A. Alvarez tells the story of Jacques Vaché, a bizarre young poet who had a decisive influence on André Breton, the founder of surrealism. Vaché was convinced of the utter futility of life and adopted as his guiding principle what he called *umore*—a malignant and self-destructive irony. He was conscripted into the French army during the First World War. In a letter from the front he explained that he objected to being killed in the war, adding, 'I shall die when I want to die, and then I shall die with somebody else. To die alone is boring. I should prefer to die with one of my best friends.'[2] In 1919, when the war was over, Vaché died in accordance with these specifications. He invited two friends to take an opium 'trip' with him. He administered a lethal dose to his unsuspecting friends and an equally lethal dose to himself. He thus did not die alone.[3]

It should be pointed out in passing that Vaché was using the expres-

1. David Hume, 'My Own Life,' reprinted in *Hume's Dialogues Concerning Natural Religion*, ed. Norman Kemp Smith (Edinburgh, 1935), p. 239. The same volume contains the letter from Adam Smith to William Strahan describing Hume's last months. Both these documents are also reprinted in *The Letters of David Hume*, ed. J. Y. T. Greig, vol. 2 (Oxford, 1932). The last-mentioned book contains the remarkable letter from Hume to Edward Gibbon upon reading the first volume of *The Decline and Fall of the Roman Empire*, which appeared while Hume was dying.

2. A. Alvarez, *The Savage God* (London and New York: Weidenfeld and Nicholson, 1971), p. 190.

3. Vaché was twenty-three when he killed himself. There is much interesting information about him in Hans Richter, *Dada* (London and New York, 1965), on which Alvarez's account is based, and in Maurice Nadeau, *The History of Surrealism* (London: Cape, 1968).

sion 'dying alone' in a confusing and improper way. If his two friends had been saved, it would have been correct to say that he, alone of the three, died and not that he died alone. 'Alone' is here equivalent to 'only', and it qualifies 'he' and not 'dying'. However, let us waive this point and accept Vaché's way of talking as a third sense in which one may speak of human beings as dying alone. Clearly, as in the case of the other two senses, some human beings die alone in this sense, and some do not. If only one of a dozen hostages is executed, he dies alone. If all or several of them are executed at the same time, they do not die alone. As before, the assertion that all human beings die alone is seen to be false.

It should be noted that the Heideggerians do not base their statement 'All men die alone' on detailed inspections of the last moments of human beings. As *they* use the expression 'dying alone' we can *deduce* that a person died alone from the mere fact that he died. No inquiry whatever is needed into the circumstances of his death. If he died, surrounded by other human beings to whom he had deep emotional ties, he nevertheless died alone simply because he died. This gives us a clue as to what has happened here. 'Dying alone' has been redefined so as to be logically equivalent to 'dying'. As the Heideggerians use 'alone' (or rather as it must be interpreted if their statement is not to be plainly false), it is *logically* impossible for a person to die and not to die alone. If 'alone' had some additional content, it would be possible to describe what it would be like for a person to die without dying alone; but, as the Heideggerians use these words, such a description is not possible. The way in which they write suggests that the logical relation between 'dying' and 'dying alone' is like the relation between 'dying' and 'dying in poverty' or 'dying' and 'dying in bed'. In both these cases we clearly have a synthetic relation: 'dying in poverty' means more than 'dying' and the same is true of 'dying in bed'. The same is also true of 'dying alone' in any of the three senses mentioned earlier, but it is not true of 'dying alone' as the Heideggerians must use this expression if their statement that everybody dies alone is not to be false. As they are committed to using these words, the relation between 'dying' and 'dying alone' is like the relation between 'father' and 'parent'. The upshot of our discussion is that if the Heideggerian statement is interpreted in such a way that it says something interesting, then it is clearly false; and if it is interpreted so as to make it true, it becomes nothing more than a rhetorical way of asserting the exceedingly familiar fact that everybody dies someday. The triviality of the

Heideggerian doctrine is not at once apparent to everybody only because, in any of its familiar senses, 'dying alone' *does* mean more than 'dying' and because the reader has not been warned (and the Heideggerians themselves have probably not realized) that 'alone' has been redefined.

The emptiness of the Heideggerian doctrine, what may not unfairly be described as its bogus character, becomes particularly clear when one reflects that it *seems* to, but does not in fact, have any practical implications. Let us suppose that a 'believer' in this 'theory' has a wife and children to whom he is attached in much the same way as non-Heideggerians have been attached to their wives and children. Let us suppose that he has an accident and is taken to a hospital. He has reason to believe that he may die very shortly. If the word 'alone' were used in any of its familiar senses in the Heideggerian statement 'all human beings die alone' and if the statement were true, then our Heideggerian should *not* send for his family. This would be entirely pointless since all human beings die alone. In practice he would send for his wife and children just like any other reasonably normal human being. In other words, acceptance of the doctrine is entirely compatible with all the usual distinctions between dying alone and not dying alone; and our Heideggerian, if he has normal human impulses, will not want to be alone but with those he loves.

Some readers are likely to object to the above criticisms that, although not everybody may be *dying* alone, it is nevertheless true, and necessarily true, that *in death* everybody is alone. These are the very words used by the translators of *Sein und Zeit* in an explanatory footnote in which they assert and apparently regard it as self-evident that 'in death Dasein is cut off from relations with others' (*BT*, p. 294n). Such a rejoinder will seem plausible to all who are under the influence of the picture of death as a kind of sleep or rest. Proust somewhere speaks of 'the mind's inability, when it ponders death, to picture something other than life,' and I think it is true that, while part of the time we know perfectly well that the dead are not sleeping or resting (i.e., alive, but in a very passive sort of way), at other times we do think of them as sleeping in the grave or as somehow continuing to exist in a dark abode.[1] If a dead

---

1. For a detailed discussion of this notion, implicit in many of our ordinary sayings about death, see the first section of my article 'Existentialism and Death: A Survey of Some Confusions and Absurdities,' in *Philosophy, Science and Method: Essays in Honor of Ernest Nagel*, ed. Sidney Morgenbesser, Patrick Suppes, and Morton White (New York: St. Martin's Press, 1969). Hereafter cited as ED.

person were indeed sleeping in his grave, he would presumably be alone, both because nobody else is in the coffin with him, and, more fundamentally, because, unlike the living, he would be incapable of communicating with anybody. A little sober reflection will show that this rejoinder is absurd. The dead are not resting or sleeping. Sleep and rest are states of *living* organisms. The statement that somebody is alone presupposes that he is alive; and while it is intelligible, though it may not be true, to say about a *dying* person that he is alone, it is nonsense to say that a *dead* man is alone.

THE UNTRANSFERABILITY OF DEATH

Death is not only Dasein's nonrelational possibility. It is also its 'ownmost possibility'. 'With death,' writes Heidegger, 'Dasein stands before itself in its ownmost potentiality-for-being' (*BT*, p. 294). This ownmost and nonrelational possibility 'is at the same time the uttermost one' (ibid.). 'Ownmost' is the word M-R use to translate the German *eigenst*, which literally means 'most my own'. If we adopt a completely literal translation, Heidegger is asserting that my death is more mine than anything else; and it is not surprising to find Father Demske telling us that death 'is the most intimate . . . possibility of one's own existence'[1] and Glen Gray speaking of death as 'this most private . . . possibility'[2] and 'the most intimate experience of all.'[3]

At first sight this sounds like mere gibberish. In one sense death is not 'mine' at all. As we shall see in detail in the next section, Heidegger and his disciples constantly confuse death with our thoughts and emotions about death. My thoughts and emotions about death are indeed 'mine', but it is difficult to see why they should be regarded as 'more mine' than, for example, my desire to love and be loved or my desire to enjoy life. Heidegger appears to be under the spell of some nebulous picture which he is also trying to foist on his readers—a picture of death concealed deep inside every one of us. However, this is not all he is doing. The statement that death is our ownmost possibility appears to be a summary of some-

---

1. *BMD*, p. 37.
2. PD, p. 56.
3. Ibid., p. 62.

thing he had defended with some feeling earlier in the same chapter, namely, that, as his followers have frequently put it, death is 'untransfer-able.' About ten pages before first using the word 'ownmost', Heidegger refers to those 'possibilities' in which one Dasein *can* represent another:

> Indisputably, the fact that one Dasein can be *represented* by another belongs to its possibilities of Being in Being-with-one-another in the world. In everyday concern, constant and manifold use is made of such representability. Whenever we go anywhere or have anything to contribute, we can be represented by someone within the range of that "environment" with which we are most closely concerned.
>
> Representability is not only quite possible but is even constitutive for our being with one another. *Here* one Dasein can and must, within certain limits, "*be*" another Dasein. (*BT*, pp. 283–84, Heidegger's italics)

In the case of death, on the other hand, no such substituting or repre-senting is possible:

> However, this possibility of representing breaks down completely if the issue is one of representing that possibility-of-Being which makes up Dasein's coming to an end. (*BT*, p. 284)

Again:

> Dying . . . is essentially mine in such a way that no one can be my representa-tive. (*BT*, p. 297)

> Death *is* always one's own. (*BT*, p. 309, G p. 265, Heidegger's italics)[1]

Disciples from different parts of the world have enthusiastically endorsed these remarks. Heinrich Knittermeyer, the author of one of the first his-torical surveys of existentialism, is emphatic that in death a human being cannot be 'replaced.' Nobody, he goes on, can 'absolve somebody else from dying. . . . Death occurs only in the singular.'[2] Johannes Pfeiffer, another German admirer, assures us that 'anxiety in the face of death, so

---

1. The German original is 'Tod *ist* je nur eigener.' M-R mistranslate this as 'Death is just one's own.' The word 'je', which is short for *jeweils*, means 'always' and not 'just'.

2. Heinrich Knittermeyer, *Die Philosophie der Existenz* (Vienna, 1952), pp. 258–59. Although Knittermeyer greatly admires both Jaspers and Sartre, he insists that neither of them can be compared with Heidegger as regards 'originality of thinking or formulation' (p. 207).

far from degrading a human being, liberates him and brings him his true dignity. . . . For death is always his own; in relation to his death no individual human being can be represented by another.'[1] J. L. Mehta, an Indian devotee who has had 'the privilege of meeting and talking with Professor Heidegger more than once in his own house,' and whose stupendous aggregation of paraphrases, *The Philosophy of Martin Heidegger*, has been hailed by other Heideggerians as 'one of the finest books to appear on Heidegger in any language,' is in total agreement. 'No deputizing,' he writes, 'is possible when it comes to that possibility of being which consists of the coming-to-an-end of Dasein and which endows it with its wholeness.'[2] None of Heidegger's American supporters voice any dissent on this topic. Death, according to John Wild, 'is not a replaceable, interchangeable function.'[3] Death, in the words of Glenn Gray, 'is unshareable. . . . It is always and ever my own. . . . No one can take my place in death, nor can I, in this sense, ever die for another.'[4] 'Death,' writes Schrag, 'is indelibly my own and therefore non-transferable. . . . No substitution of roles is possible when it comes to dying.'[5] 'If there is anything that is my own,' Gelven exclaims, 'it is my death. . . . Every man dies his own death. It cannot be shared or be taken over by someone else.'[6] 'Though another man may die in my place,' writes William H. Bossart, 'another can never die my death.'[7] 'My death,' to quote William Barrett, 'is essentially mine.'[8]

It is important to point out that, in one fairly obvious sense, it is not true that one cannot, ever or in principle, get somebody else to die in one's place. In Schiller's poem 'Die Bürgschaft' (The Bond) the tyrant, Dionys, sentences Möros to death by crucifixion for attempting to assas-

---

1. Johannes Pfeiffer, *Existenzphilosophie*, 2nd ed. (Hamburg, 1949), p. 26.

2. This passage is quoted from p. 228 of the complete Indian edition of 1967, published in Varanasi by Banaras Hindu University Press. The remark about Mehta's meetings with Heidegger is taken from p. xix of the preface to the abbreviated American edition (New York: Harper & Row, 1971). The praise of Mehta comes from Jack D. Caputo, *Review of Metaphysics* (1973): 760–61.

3. *CE*, p. 239.

4. *PD*, pp. 54–55.

5. *EF*, p. 114.

6. *CBT*, pp. 150, 142.

7. 'Three Directions of Phenomenology,' in *The Anatomy of Knowledge*, ed. M. Grene (Amherst: University of Massachusetts Press, 1969), p. 270. In fairness it should be added that, although Bossart treats Heidegger with great respect, unlike the other writers quoted here, he does not appear to be an uncritical admirer.

8. William Barrett, 'The Listener,' February 16, 1978, p. 202.

sinate him. Möros begs for three days' grace to get his sister married off. Dionys agrees on condition that Möros's best friend remain behind as a hostage. If Möros does not return in time the friend is to die in his place. An interesting actual case of this kind involving Thomas Paine occurred during the French Revolution. Paine was at that time an exile from England, where the government had ordered a warrant for his arrest and also instigated an unbelievably vicious campaign of slander and vilification. Although he was himself later condemned to death, in the earlier stages of the Revolution Paine was a deputy in the Constituent Assembly and exercised considerable influence. An Englishman by the name of Zachariah Wilkes had been condemned for another's offense. Wilkes appealed to Paine for help, although, as he put it, 'Paine must hate and detest the name of any Englishman—pelted, insulted, persecuted and slandered' as he had been by the English government. Paine had Wilkes released and stood as hostage in his place while Wilkes went to England. Paine's confidence was not abused. Wilkes returned in time with proof of his innocence. In these cases the hostages did not in fact die in the place of the people they represented, but they easily might have done so. In principle a substitution of this kind is entirely possible, and there is no doubt that, in the sense just explained, people have on occasion died in the place of other human beings.

Heidegger is aware of these facts, but he dismisses them as irrelevant to his point: '*No one can take the Other's dying away from him.* Of course someone can "go to his death for another." But that always means to sacrifice oneself for the Other "*in some definite affair.*" Such "dying for" can never signify that the Other has thus been delivered from his death in even the slightest degree. Dying is something that every Dasein itself must take upon itself at the time. By its very essence, death is in every case mine, in so far as it "is" at all' (*BT*, p. 286, G p. 249; Heidegger's italics). It is evident that Heidegger ends up with two statements that are not affected by the occurrence or the possibility of the kind of substitution we discussed in the last paragraph. They are, first, the statement that nobody can die another's death, i.e., that the death a person dies is his and not somebody else's, and second, the statement that although one person can sacrifice himself for another, he cannot *ultimately* deliver him from his death, i.e., prevent him from dying.

It seems to me that both of these statements are true but that both of them are trite, though for different reasons. The first is what we may call a 'grammatical' truth. It in effect simply states a rule of language. It tells us that if there are two human beings or for that matter two animals or living beings of any kind, A and B, then if A dies it is incorrect to say that A dies B's death and vice versa. The statement that nobody can die another's death appears to assert a certain fact, a certain limitation or incapacity of human beings. In this it seems to be like the statement that no human being can run a hundred yards in less than five seconds or that no human being can indefinitely resist the kind of torture to which the defendants in the notorious Trotsky trials were subjected in the Soviet Union in the 1930s. The latter statements are true, if they are true, because of certain facts. Heidegger's statement similarly seems to assert the existence of certain physical or psychological limitations. In fact, however, it does nothing of the kind. The reason why I cannot die somebody else's death has nothing to do with physical or psychological limitations. It is the same as the reason why if I have gout, it must be my own gout and not somebody else's or why if I have a cramp in my right foot, the cramp must be mine and not the cramp of George W. Bush or of Nancy Reagan or of any other human being. To say that I have a cramp in my foot includes as part of what I am asserting that the cramp is mine. This is not an extra fact, over and above the fact that I have a cramp. Exactly the same applies to the statement that I will die. It includes as part of its content that the death I will die is mine. The explicit statement of a rule of language is not necessarily trite; it may be important and illuminating if it is a rule that is not always obeyed and if violation of the rule leads to confused theorizing. However, in the present case there is no reason to believe that anybody has ever had the slightest tendency to go against the rule in question. When President Kennedy died, it did not occur to anybody, including the most inauthentic nonexistentialist, to say that President Kennedy died the death of Richard Nixon or the death of Barry Goldwater or the death of anybody other than his own. It is clear that when William Barrett said that his death was 'essentially' his, he erred on the side of moderation. Our linguistic rules guarantee that when Barrett dies, his death will be his, not just 'essentially' but utterly, totally, and without qualification.

The statement that ultimately nobody can deliver somebody else from dying is also trite, but for a different reason. It is a factual statement and not the formulation of a rule of language, but in effect it asserts nothing more than that ultimately everybody dies. It is important to insert here the word 'ultimately' because, nonultimately, other people may 'deliver' me from my death, in the way explained earlier. *Ultimately* they cannot deliver me from my death, but this is so because ultimately I am going to die. Heidegger's statement does not assert any fact over and above the fact that I am going to die; it simply reasserts this fact and hence it is not a discovery or an insight or a contribution to our understanding of anything.

There is a relatively easy explanation why Heidegger's untransferability doctrine *seems* to amount to more than the two trite statements just discussed. It seems to come to more because, after admitting that the initial claim of untransferability is false in the sense in which it is most naturally construed, Heidegger nevertheless retains the original language. Let us distinguish between the following three statements:

1. In the matter of death no human being can substitute for another.
2. The death a person dies is and must be his own.
3. Nobody can ultimately deliver another human being from dying.

Unlike 2 and 3, 1, as it is most naturally understood, is not trite. It makes a most interesting claim—the claim that, unlike in such matters as lecturing or singing an operatic role or treating a patient or defending a client in a criminal case, representation or substitution is not possible when it comes to dying. In practice this would mean that a lecturer can, at least in principle, get somebody else to take his place, that singers, doctors, and lawyers can get substitutes for their respective professional jobs, but that it is *in principle* impossible to get somebody else to die in one's place. This claim, if true, would be most interesting; but we have seen that it is not true. Heidegger acknowledges this and shifts to 2 and 3. However, he retains the initial language, suggesting quite falsely that 1 has been vindicated.

It will be worthwhile to show in some detail that, as far as 'representability' or 'substitutability' is concerned, there is a strict parallel between dying on the one hand and such activities as lecturing, performing in an opera, treating patients, or defending a person on the other. For this purpose I will imagine a strange and perverted land, called

'Clockwork Orange', in which there is a society of psychotic sadists known as 'the Torturers'. This society has been granted a special charter by the government allowing them to put to death one person at their meeting on the first Monday evening of every month. The one condition is that the individual they decide to kill must never have offended any member of that society. Once they pick their victim, the police are instructed to deliver him alive. Let us suppose that I have been picked for next Monday and the government has issued a warrant for my arrest. The Torturers decided that this time they wanted a professional philosopher, and they randomly selected me from a list of members of the Philosophical Association of Clockwork Orange. Let us furthermore suppose that I have a devoted assistant, also a professional philosopher, by the name of Samuel Blau, who has often substituted for me in my classes at the leading adult education school in Clockwork Orange, the New School for Humanistic Studies. I don't particularly want to die next Monday, not because I have anything against death, but because I am in the middle of an article on Heidegger which I don't want to leave unfinished. I therefore ask Samuel Blau if he would be so kind as to substitute for me, and he readily agrees. I call the secretary of the Torturers, who does not object so long as Blau is also a professional philosopher, which I assure him he is. Finally, the chief of police agrees to the substitution. Blau is thereupon apprehended and killed at the Monday meeting. Now, I wish to insist that Blau's substitution for me in the matter of dying is, in all relevant respects, *exactly* parallel to his substituting for me at the New School for Humanistic Studies. He substituted at the New School by lecturing and discussing the topic that I would have discussed if I had gone in. He produced certain effects upon the students analogous to those I would have produced. He substitutes for me at the Monday meeting of the Torturers by doing or suffering what I would have done or suffered, and he produces effects on the audience (presumably of sadistic delight) analogous to those which my dying would have produced. If somebody now says, 'But he would die his death and not yours,' this is true but irrelevant— irrelevant to the fact of his substituting for me. He also did not give my lecture; or, assuming that I had written it out and he merely read it, his reading of the lecture was *his* and not mine. If somebody then maintains, 'But his appearing at the Monday meeting of the Torturers does not prevent you from eventually dying,' the answer is again that this is true but irrelevant. It has nothing to whatever to do with the fact of his substituting for me on that occasion. It is no more relevant than if somebody had said, 'Sam Blau did not really substitute for you at the New School last Tuesday because although he showed up and gave a most interesting lecture on the topic you were supposed to cover, he will not substitute for you in all your future classes.' But, it will be said, ultimately neither Blau nor anybody else can prevent me from dying, while in principle somebody else can substitute for all the lectures I will ever be scheduled to give. This is true, but once more irrelevant. It shows that Heidegger's proposition 3 is true. It does not show that Blau did not represent me at the meeting of the Torturers in *exactly* the same sense in which he represented me at the New School; and more generally it does not show in the slightest that death is untransferable in the only natural sense of the word. Just like Heidegger's procedure, this retort involves a shift from the interesting but false assertion 1 to the true but platitudinous statement 3.

The upshot of our discussion is that the untransferability doctrine is true in senses in which it is trite and false in the sense in which it would be interesting. It seems both interesting and true only if the shift which I have been describing is not clearly noticed.

BEING-TOWARDS-DEATH

All major existentialists who have written about death (with the one notable exception of Sartre) oppose their own teaching on the subject to what they refer as the 'external' view of death. This is a view shared by the pagan philosophers of antiquity, by Hegel and his disciples, by naturalistic philosophers of the twentieth century, and also by most non-philosophers when they think about death. On this view, as Schrag has put it, death is an 'external and objective phenomenon,'[1] it is 'simply a natural and empirical happening which comes to man at the completion of his life.'[2] This 'external' view is typically represented by the saying of Epicurus: 'When I am, death is not and when death is, I am not.' It is also implicit in the 'common' notion of 'death as that which results when one

---

1. *EF*, p. 100.
2. Ibid., p. 113.

takes a dose of sulfuric acid, or drowns himself, or goes to sleep in an atmosphere of coal gas.'[1] Such an external point of view of death is radically defective. 'Classical paganism,' Schrag tells us, 'never arrives at a *genuine understanding* of the *existential reality* of death.' Like 'Hegel's objective idealism' it fails to achieve 'subjective penetration' of death. The same is true of the everyday conception of death: 'In our common, everyday, leveled understanding, what is existentially involved in dying fails to become transparent.'[2] Viewing death as an 'external fact' does not yield a 'proper understanding.'[3] The assumption that it is 'simply a natural and empirical happening' is *'false.'*[4] William Barrett is in total agreement with this assessment of the 'everyday understanding' of death. People 'usually think of death as a fact in the world. . . . It is something out there in the world as yet external to me.' This is a mistake: 'Death is not a public fact out there in the world.'[5] In opposition to this external view we are assured that Kierkegaard, Heidegger, and other existentialists have achieved a proper understanding of death. They have done so by 'interiorizing' death, to quote Schrag, by showing that death is an 'interior possibility of the human self as concern or passion.'[6] 'Existentialist thinkers agree that death can be elucidated and described as a constitutive structure in man's situationality.'[7] Heidegger in particular has developed an 'ontology of death' in which 'death is *"interiorized"* as a mode of existence itself.'[8] Thanks to Heidegger, writes Father Demske, we realize that death is an *'internal* existential structure of the being of Dasein.'[9] 'Death,' furthermore, 'is not an event which puts an end to life. . . . It does not lie in the future, but in the here and now, affecting every act in which existence is realized.'[10] 'Death as an existential is . . . a mode of being, a way to be, in fact *the* way in which Dasein exists.'[11] 'Death,' according to Glenn Gray, 'is a phenomenon within life,' and he adds that 'if it is taken

1. *EF*, pp. 102–103.
2. Ibid., p. 102, my italics.
3. Ibid., p. 103.
4. Ibid., p. 113, my italics.
5. *WE*, p. 63.
6. *EF*, p. 98.
7. Ibid., p. 96.
8. Ibid., p. 95, Schrag's italics.
9. *BMD*, p. 72, my italics.
10. Ibid., p. 7.
11. Ibid., p. 25, Demske's italics.

into life in a personal way, it will effect a revolution in our behavior.'[1] 'Death,' writes Father Boros, 'is a *fundamental modality of living.*'[2] 'The peculiar thing,' Barrett remarks, is that 'my death will never be a fact in the world for me.' He goes on to observe that he will never read his own obituary and tells us that he regards this as a 'very significant fact.' Since death is not something 'out there in the world,' it is an 'interior possibility,'[3] it is 'something that happens *within* my own existence.'[4]

How is the feat of 'interiorizing' death accomplished? How is it shown that death is not external, but 'internal,' that it is 'a mode of life'? This result, which on the face of it seems quite remarkable, is obtained by an analysis of what are claimed to be the different senses of the word 'end' and the corresponding senses of 'dying'. It is 'urgent,' Heidegger tells us, to 'ask *in what sense, if any, death must be conceived as the ending of Dasein*' (*BT*, p. 289, Heidegger's italics). To answer this question it is necessary to discuss the different senses of 'ending'. Schrag, who goes into somewhat more detail here than Heidegger, observes that 'to come to an end commonly means to cease,' adding however that '"ceasing to be" has different modifications.'[5] One such 'modification' or sense is illustrated by Heidegger's own example—'the rain has stopped'. Schrag gives the example of the end of the summer. Here we have 'disappearance'—that which has ended, the rain or the summer is, in Heidegger's special terminology, 'no longer present-at-hand' (*BT*, p. 289). In another sense, ending means completion. An artist has come to the end of his work when he has completed a painting 'with the last stroke of the brush' (*BT*, p. 289). A further 'modification' of ending is provided by cases where work will never be completed, in Schrag's words, 'as when construction of a canal stops because the soil through which it must be cut proves too swampy.'[6] A fourth modification is exemplified when something is used up, for example, a supply of gasoline or when we come to the end of a loaf of bread. Heidegger mentions another case which is significantly different from all those listed so far. If we come to the end of the road, this does not imply that the road has disappeared. Unlike the

1. PD, p. 53.
2. *MT*, p. 8, Boros's italics.
3. Barrett, 'The Listener.'
4. *WE*, p. 63, my italics.
5. *EF*, p. 112.
6. Ibid., p. 112.

gasoline that has been used up, the bread that has been eaten, or the rain that has stopped, the road continues to exist. 'Such an ending,' writes Heidegger, 'does not make the road disappear, but . . . is determinative for the road as this one, which is present-at-hand' (*BT*, p. 289). There is some talk about 'fulfillment' at this stage. It is not clear whether Heidegger regards fulfillment as a 'mode' of what he calls *fertigwerden* which M-R translate as 'finishedness' and which in ordinary German simply means 'completion'. 'Fulfilling,' Heidegger writes, 'is a mode of "finishedness," and is founded upon it.' However, both he and Schrag insist—and rightly so—that ending in the sense of finishedness or completion does not necessarily involve fulfillment. 'A project,' to quote Schrag, 'may end in the sense of being completed and yet be evaluated as either fulfilled or unfulfilled, as when we say that a performance ended well or ended poorly.'[1]

In which of these senses does the death of Dasein constitute its end? In none of them. Many readers will be familiar with the basic distinction which Heidegger makes between Dasein on the one hand and entities that are ready-to-hand and present-at-hand on the other. This distinction is similar to the one between persons and things which is found in the thought of many nonexistentialists, and it closely corresponds to Sartre's distinction between the *pour-soi* and the *en-soi*. Human beings have certain characteristics which are not possessed by inanimate objects or by plants and animals; and they are called Daseins to indicate their possession of these characteristics. Now, it is Heidegger's contention that the senses, modes, or modifications of 'ending' previously enumerated apply only to non-Daseins. Human beings are radically different from bread, paintings, roads, and the rain; and their end is radically different from the end of all these other entities: '*By none of these modes of ending can death be suitably characterized as the "end" of Dasein.* If dying, as Being-at-an-end, were understood in the sense of an ending of the kind we have discussed, then Dasein would thereby be treated as something present-at-hand or ready-at-hand. In death, Dasein has not been fulfilled nor has it simply disappeared; it has not become finished nor is it wholly at one's disposal as something ready-to-hand' (p. 289, Heidegger's italics). The 'modifications of ending' so far discussed, in Schrag's words, 'are not applicable to the unique Being of *Dasein* and hence cannot be used to characterize death as the end of his being-in-the-world.'

---

1. *EF*, p. 112.

In what sense is death the end of Dasein? To answer this question we must briefly explain one of the key notions of *BT*—'existentiality' or 'running-ahead' (*vorlaufen*), what Schrag calls 'protention'. Human beings, according to Heidegger, are always 'ahead' of themselves in the sense that they are and cannot help being concerned about their future. To explain the behavior or motion of inanimate objects and most, if not all, living things other than man, we need not take into account their concern for the future, since they have no such concern. In the case of human beings, on the other hand, we cannot understand their *present* behavior or states without taking into account their concern for the future. Perhaps I should remark in passing that, although I object to various uses to which this notion is put by Heidegger, I do not at all dispute the fact that human beings are characterized by existentiality or *vorlaufen*. If we keep in mind this universal characteristic of *vorlaufen*, Heidegger maintains, we shall discover the peculiar sense, radically different from all the other senses, in which death is the end of Dasein:

> The "ending" which we have in view when we speak of death, does not signify Dasein's Being-at-an-end but a *Being-towards-the-end* of this entity. (p. 289, Heidegger's italics)

> *Death is*, as Dasein's end, *in* the Being of this entity *towards* its end. (p. 303, my italics of 'in', otherwise Heidegger's italics)

It is in the 'protentional character of Dasein' or its 'running-ahead,' Schrag tells us, 'that the phenomenon of death is disclosed.' This yields an 'existential understanding' of death and 'existentially understood, death does not signify a being-at-the-end.' The 'existentialist clarification of the meaning of the end' allows us to regard 'death as being-unto-the-end.'[1] 'For the subjective thinker,' death 'is a present reality.'[2] 'Death is a mode of human concern . . . in which the transitoriness of existence is disclosed.'[3]

Heidegger appears to believe that, in a quite literal sense, a human being *is* already its future, its 'not-yet'; and thus he finds no difficulty in concluding that Dasein's end is already present while he is alive:

---

1. *EF*, p. 113.
2. Ibid., p. 108.
3. Ibid., p. 97.

Just as Dasein *is* already its "not-yet," and is its "not-yet" constantly as long as it is, it *is* already its end too. (p. 289, Heidegger's italics)

Death "is not something to which Dasein ultimately comes only in its demise. In Dasein, as being towards its death, its own uttermost "not-yet" has already been included." (p. 303)

Dasein, furthermore, "stretches *itself* along in such a way that its own Being is constituted in advance as a stretching along." (p. 426)

In this way, by means of running-ahead and 'stretching' (*erstrecken*), Dasein can encompass its entire future. It can 'take in advance' (*vorwegnehmen*) the rest of its life and it can thus catch up with (*einholen*) its own death: 'Since running-ahead to the possibility which is not to be outstripped discloses also all the possibilities which lie ahead of that possibility [meaning all future events that will happen before one's death], this running-ahead includes the possibility of taking *the whole* of Dasein in advance' (*BT*, p. 309, G p. 264, Heidegger's italics). Needless to say, this 'amalgamation' of present and future has the wholehearted endorsement of various of Heidegger's disciples. 'The not-yet element of human existence,' in the words of Gelven, 'is something that is already there. Dasein is, in a very genuine sense, already its not-yet.' 'Dasein's "not-yet death",' furthermore, 'is already available for inquiry in a living and existing Dasein.'[1] Similarly, Schrag assures us that 'the existential future is *already* present . . . nor is the future a thing which will become real during the "course of time" at a later date. The future is already real.'[2] Again: 'In existential anticipation (vorlaufen) the future is brought into the present.'[3] 'Dasein as ecstatic existence is stretched out into . . . a future in which he *already* is.'[4] 'The future,' according to Glenn Gray, 'can be liberated if it is conceived as part of the present. . . . The future will be seen to belong to the present in a fundamental way. . . . The future must be regarded in a new way, as part of

---

1. *CBT*, p. 147.
2. *EF*, p. 127.
3. Ibid., p. 141.
4. Ibid., p. 146, Schrag's italics.

the existential moment. . . . We understand the term "future" as a dimension of the present.'[1]

Heidegger repeatedly remarks that *all* human beings are dying *all the time*. 'Factically,' he writes, 'one's own Dasein is always dying' (p. 292). 'Factically, Dasein is dying as long as it exists' (p. 295). And most fully: 'Dasein is dying factically and indeed constantly, as long as it has not yet come to its demise' (p. 303). Clearly, these statements are another way of expressing the doctrine that human life is being-towards-death. When Heidegger asserts that all human beings are dying all the time he is not referring to the fact that cells are constantly dying in human bodies. Heidegger is not concerned with such biological details. That the life of human beings is being-towards-death is something that could have been known (and I suppose Heidegger would say was in fact known, though not in the explicit way in which *BT* codifies this knowledge) long before biologists knew that cells are constantly dying and even long before the existence of cells had been discovered. Biological facts Heidegger would classify as 'ontic'. That human life is being-towards-death is something 'ontological'. Although the meaning of 'ontological' is never clearly explained, it is apparent that Heidegger would not regard a characteristic of human beings as 'ontological' if it were not somehow necessarily connected with or part of the constitution of their humanity; and being-towards-death is essentially connected with their humanity, while any detailed facts discovered by biologists are not.

The remarks of the preceding paragraph tell us what 'dying' in the existential or ontological sense does not mean. They do not tell us what it does mean; and I do not think that any of the passages quoted from Heidegger or Schrag or Demske spell out very clearly the content of 'being-towards-death'. To discover this we have to determine the necessary and sufficient conditions which an entity must satisfy in order for its life to be characterized as being-towards-death. Clearly one condition is that an entity should die in the biological sense. As I understand Heidegger, the life of human beings would definitely not be being-towards-death if they lived forever in the biological sense. However, this condition is clearly not enough. For Heidegger and his followers are emphatic that the life of

---

1. PD, pp. 59–60.

plants and animals is not being-towards-death, although they also die in the biological sense.[1]

What is true of human beings and not true of plants and animals in virtue of which we attribute being-towards-death to the former and not to the latter? Some of Heidegger's remarks in this connection are enigmatic, but various of his followers have been more explicit, and it is, I think, fairly easy to see the kind of thing he has in mind. 'Non-human organisms,' in the words of Father Demske, 'actually come to an end, but assume no attitude or relation to their cessation and thus have no "being-unto-the-end."'[2] Similarly, in a passage previously quoted, Schrag speaks of being-towards-death as a mode of 'concern.' Human beings, to begin with, know that they are going to die in a sense in which animals and plants do not know this. It is often said that animals have an instinctive fear of death, but even if this is so it is not the same thing as explicit awareness of death; and it is certainly not the same thing as what Heidegger is specially concerned with when he talks about anxiety as contrasted with fear, namely the realization that death means total extinction or 'utter nullity.' The knowledge human beings have of their mortality has or may have all kinds of significant effects on their behavior and on their emotions. In short, unlike animals and plants, they think about their death, they are concerned about their death, and, sometimes at least, they act in ways in which they would not have acted if they had not known their own mortality. It should be emphasized that, according to Heidegger, being-towards-death is not something we can help. It is not in any sense within our volitional control. What is within our volitional control is whether our being-

---

1. In addition to distinguishing between biological death and death in the 'existential' sense, which is being-towards-death, Heidegger distinguishes two different senses of biological death. The former of these he calls '*Verenden*', and the latter '*Ableben*', which M-R translate as 'perish' and 'demise', respectively. Plants and animals 'perish.' Dasein never perishes. It 'demises' (p. 291). '*Ableben*', or 'demising', according to Schrag, 'refers to the biological termination of human life or man's ontic annihilation.' I assume that the distinction between 'perishing' and 'demising' is meant to do justice to the fact that human beings are in a sense more than biological organisms, that they are conscious beings and that their death involves the end of their mental and not only of their physical existence. I am not sure that this is what is meant because the higher animals, too, are conscious beings and also because talking in this way implies a dualism to which Heidegger seems to be opposed elsewhere in *BT*. Without denying the various differences between human beings on the one hand and plants and animals on the other, I do not see that we have here two different senses of biological 'death' or two different senses of 'ending'. I shall say more about this last topic at the end of the present section.

2. *BMD*, p. 95.

towards-death is to be 'authentic' or 'inauthentic.' 'Dasein has always *decided* itself in one way or another' (p. 303, my italics). Most commonly, Dasein's comportment towards death is of the inauthentic kind. 'Proximally and for the most part Dasein covers up its ownmost Being-towards-death, fleeing *in the face of it*' (p. 295, Heidegger's italics). This 'everyday falling evasion *in the face of* death is an *inauthentic* Being-towards-death' (p. 303, Heidegger's italics). Such evasive comportment, however, is no less a form of Being-towards-death than the authentic variety: 'In thus falling and fleeing *in the face of* death, Dasein's everydayness attests that the very "they" itself already has the definite character of *Being-towards-death*, even when it is not explicitly engaged in "thinking about death"' (pp. 298–99, Heidegger's italics). Death is 'constantly an issue for Dasein' even in 'average everydayness' (p. 299). 'Everyday Dasein,' no less than authentic Dasein, '*is towards its end*—that is to say, is constantly coming to grips with its death, though in a "fugitive" manner' (p. 303, Heidegger's italics). Being-towards-death is not something which Dasein 'procures for itself . . . occasionally in the course of its Being' (p. 295). It characterizes Dasein right from the start. 'It belongs essentially to Dasein's thrownness, which reveals itself in a state-of-mind in one way or another' (ibid.).

The above account makes it clear that all that is meant by the Heideggerian statement that human life is being-towards-death is, first, that human beings die, and, second, that unlike plants and animals they know and are, fugitively or nonfugitively, concerned about their death. The objection to this statement is not that it is false but that it is a platitude. Heidegger and his disciples announce this doctrine with the kind of fanfare that is usually reserved for a major contribution to human knowledge. The impression is given that it constitutes a great discovery or an important insight; and we are given to understand that Heidegger has refuted or at least corrected the view of the pagan thinkers of antiquity, of naturalistic philosophers, and of ordinary people, that death is an 'external' fact. It is easy to show that Heidegger's doctrine is not a discovery of anything, that it embodies no significant insight, and that it does not in any way refute or correct the view that death is an 'external' fact. It states what are for the most part exceedingly familiar facts which are not disputed by pagans, naturalists, or ordinary people, but it states them in pretentious and fantastically misleading language. We are offered a platitude, accompanied by a slurring of certain elementary distinctions and a set of perverse redefinitions.

To show the emptiness of the Heideggerian doctrine and the perverse character of Heidegger's verbal games it will be helpful to insist on a simple distinction which no sane person disputes. This is the distinction between death (in the ordinary sense) and a knowledge of and concern about death. Death in the ordinary sense is *not* a 'way to be,' a 'mode of human concern,' or a 'mode of life.' It is the absence of life. *Knowledge and concern* about death may be a mode of life or aspects or constituents of a mode of life. While writing these words I am alive. My death is something which has not yet taken place. My concern about death occurs while I am alive, and it precedes my death. It will be convenient to use the symbol d_o to refer to death in the ordinary sense and to use c_d to refer to knowledge of and concern about one's death. We are told by Heidegger and his followers that, 'existentially' and 'properly' understood, death is being-toward-death. This 'existential' and 'proper' understanding of death is supposed to 'interiorize' death and make it into a 'present' fact. It allegedly shows the falseness or inadequacy of the naturalist view. In effect Heidegger and his followers propose to use the word 'death' in a drastically new sense to mean c_d and not d_o. If anybody wishes to talk in this way, there is no law to stop him, but one can point out that it accomplishes nothing, or nothing of any value. Referring to c_d by the word 'death' does not amount to a discovery of anything. Nor does it refute or correct the Epicurean viewpoint. In declaring 'when death is, I am not,' Epicurus spoke about d_o and not about c_d. To refute Epicurus, d_o and not c_d would have to be shown to be an 'interior' and 'present' reality; and this has not been done. Epicurus did indeed advocate an attitude towards death that is very different from the one that appears to be endorsed by Heideggerians. However, it is safe to assume that he was neither ignorant nor oblivious of the fact that, unlike plants and animals, human beings know and are concerned about their death.

Contrary to Schrag's claim, Heidegger's redefinition is not 'the elucidation' or 'clarification' of anything whatsoever. On the contrary, the undeniable difference between d_o and c_d has been slurred over and obscured. Heidegger himself cannot, of course, do without this distinction. Thus he speaks of Dasein's 'uttermost and unoutstrippable possibility,' and he says a great deal about the 'anxiety' that is involved in an 'authentic' approach to this uttermost and unoutstrippable possibility. The uttermost and unoutstrippable possibility is *death* and not *being-towards-death*; and if death were not distinguished from being-towards-death there would not be anything for the authentic approach to be an approach to. Being-towards-death is being towards *death in the ordinary sense*, i.e., towards d_o. It is *not* being towards c_d, towards death in the new, redefined or existential sense; it is being-towards-*death* and not being-towards-*being-towards*-death.

Similar comments apply to the contention of Schrag, Barrett, Gray, and other Heideggerians that death is not a public fact but something that happens 'within' a person's existence. Barrett observes that his death will not be a fact in the world *for him*, and he regards it as highly significant that he will not be around to read his obituary. All this is totally irrelevant to the point at issue between Heideggerians and Epicurus. That Barrett will not be able to witness his death or that he will not read his obituary does not have the slightest tendency to show that his death will not be a public fact. Barrett's death, when it occurs, *will* be a public fact—it will be observed, or at any rate it could in principle become the object of the observation of people who will be alive at the time. Let us divide the history of the world into three phases—the phase coinciding with Barrett's life, the pre-Barrett phase, and the post-Barrett phase. During the pre-Barrett phase a multitude of public facts existed, although Barrett was unable to observe them. Similarly, in the post-Barrett phase there will be a vast number of facts (other than his own death) whose public character will not in any way be undone by Barrett's inability to perceive them. The same is obviously true of Barrett's death. What is or may be a 'private' fact, what happens 'within' a person's existence while he is alive, is not death but thoughts and concern about death.[1]

The emptiness of the Heideggerian doctrine can be seen very clearly when we take a closer look at Heidegger's assertion that all human beings, including young people who are in the best of health and leading the safest possible life, are always dying. This certainly sounds like a discovery. It *appears* to conflict with commonly accepted beliefs, but this appearance is deceptive. Let us assume that Samuel Blau is a man of fifty-five who is dying (in the ordinary sense) of some dreadful disease like stomach cancer. Let us suppose that he has a son, Bobby, aged twenty, who appears to be in the best of health. The family physician, Dr. Adelman, is a convert to Heidegger's philosophy. Bobby has a regular checkup and Dr. Adelman finds nothing wrong with his health. Nevertheless, Dr. Adelman tells the mother, 'I am sorry to inform you that not only

---

1. I regret to note that Barrett died after this paragraph was written. To be strictly accurate some of the sentences would have to be reworded.

your husband but your son Bobby, too, is dying.' The poor startled woman calls out in dismay, 'But he looks so well and he is so young—don't tell me he, too, has cancer.' To this Dr. Adelman replies, 'No, no—he does not have cancer, he is in the best of health, but you must realize that he is going to die eventually, that he knows he is going to die and that he has some attitude, authentic or inauthentic—I am not sure which—to his death.' Bobby's mother, if she kept her composure, could appropriately reply, 'It is a relief to hear that Bobby is dying only in this special sense of yours. I just wish my husband, too, were dying only in this sense.' Dr. Adelman's statement that Bobby, too, is dying is a platitude whose platitudinous nature is not at once apparent because he is using a familiar word in an unfamiliar sense. Heidegger *seems* to be saying that everybody at *all* times is mortally ill like Samuel Blau. This indeed would be a tremendous and a shattering discovery, but it is false; and it is *not* what Heidegger really asserts. The Heideggerian physician seems to but has not in fact made a surprising discovery about Bobby; and Heidegger seems to, but has not added to our knowledge or understanding of anything when he announces that everybody is always dying.

Heidegger's argument that we do not mean the same by 'end' when we speak of the end of a human life as we do when we speak of the end of the life of a plant or an animal, or the end of an inanimate object, is totally fallacious. When we speak of the end of the latter kind of entity we mean that it ceases or has ceased to exist. We allegedly do not mean this when we speak of the end of a human life. The argument to support this conclusion rests on the contention that, unlike the other entities, human beings are Daseins—they are characterized by such features or capacities as running-ahead or existentiality. This is true, but it does not prove Heidegger's point. From the fact that human beings are Daseins it does not at once follow that a category applicable to non-Daseins is not also applicable to them; and it also does not follow that when the same word is predicated of both, it does not mean the same thing in both cases. The category of causation clearly applies to non-Daseins. It *may* be true, but it certainly does not automatically follow that, because human beings are Daseins, their actions are not caused in the same sense in which we speak of the causation of physical events and purely biological phenomena. In fact, Heidegger and Schrag notwithstanding, it is perfectly clear that when we speak of the end of a human life we use the word 'end' in exactly the same sense in which we use it when we use it when speaking of the end of non-Daseins. When a house has been wrecked or burned down, its existence has come to an end. It has ceased to exist and, barring survival after death, which is not what Heidegger and Schrag are concerned with, exactly the same is true when a human being has died. The fact that the subjects of these statements are different from one another in all kinds of ways does not mean that the word 'end' is predicated of them in different senses. Of course, if one *re*defines 'end' to mean knowledge of and concern about the end, i.e., 'being-towards-the-end', as Heidegger eventually does, then Daseins do end in a sense in which non-Daseins do not end. But this is not an elucidation of anything. It is just the same verbal trick which we already exposed in the case of the word 'death'.

Some Heideggerians seem uneasily aware of the emptiness of the doctrine under discussion, and they try to shore it up by alluding to certain additional empirical facts. Thus Father Demske quotes a passage from Karl Rahner in which the latter observes that throughout life we are 'continually disappointed, ceaselessly piercing through realities into their nothingness, continually narrowing the possibilities of free life through our actual decisions and actual life. . . . We die throughout life and what we call death is really the end of death, the death of death.'[1] Demske also quotes certain statements made by Tanabe, the Japanese Heideggerian to whom I referred earlier. Tanabe repeatedly remarks that man 'lives dying' and also 'dies living,' which Demske interprets to mean that 'during the whole of life man is constantly forced to give things up, to deny himself, do without things, offer himself.'[2] To this it must be replied that, in

---

1. *BMD*, p. 200.

2. Ibid. It should be pointed out in fairness to Tanabe that his article is not at all concerned with Demske's question. His statements that man 'lives dying' and 'dies living' are incidental to his larger themes. These include the grounding of all that is temporal and finite in the Infinite-Absolute, which is also the Eternal, the nature of the 'absolute Nothing,' and the 'concrete origin' of Heidegger's *'Ereignis'* ('Event'). Tanabe offers numerous highly illuminating remarks that should be of special interest to students of the Nothing. In connection with the 'concrete origin' of Heidegger's *'Ereignis'* Tanabe tells us that 'dialectic turns back into the Nothing as the self-negation of Being and thereby denies the identity of thinking and Being in the mode of total negation, i.e., as neither identical nor non-identical' (p. 126). A few pages later we are presented with the following pearl: 'The Absolute Nothing or the Nothing of the Nothing loves and essentially affirms all that is real' (p. 129). Philosophers who have been puzzled about the nature of freedom will be interested in Tanabe's views on the subject: 'Free choice occurs in the Nothing as a crack and [as] an empty gaping hole of the self-negation of the eternal which has been disrupted in repetition' (p. 103). Father Demske deserves special credit for rescuing this remarkable essay from oblivion.

declaring human life to be being-towards-death, Heidegger is *not* asserting any of the facts mentioned by Rahner and Tanabe. Presumably Heidegger would not deny that all or almost all human beings are occasionally disappointed, that they have to make sacrifices and deny themselves various satisfactions, but this is a purely contingent matter and would be classified by Heidegger as something 'ontic'. It is *at least* logically conceivable that a human being might go through life without once being disappointed and without having to deny himself anything. Such a person's life, as Heidegger uses the expression, would nevertheless be an instance of being-towards-death. It would be so because, in spite of his freedom from disappointments and the absence of sacrifices, he, too, would die and he, too, would know that he was going to die and adopt some kind of attitude towards his death.

A final word about the Heideggerian notion that the future *is* in the present, that I am 'already' all my not-yets, including my death. Heidegger is evidently under the spell of certain pictures—pictures associated with the words *vorlaufen, erstrecken, einholen,* and *vorwegnehmen.* I can stretch out and reach the salt shaker while I remain sitting on my chair. If I am in the front row of a procession I can run ahead and thus be in advance of the position I would be occupying if I had stayed in line. Heidegger believes that in the same way I can stretch or run into the future while I am still in the present. If this were possible, then I *could* now be my not-yet, and I could also get my death into the present. But it is not possible. Heideggerians can take this sort of talk seriously only as long as it is conducted on a totally abstract level, unrelieved by a single concrete illustration. I can now, in 2003, think about 2004 and other future years, but I cannot literally live in them. I can *metaphorically* 'run ahead' and 'stretch into' 2004, but all this means is that I can think about, prepare for, or be hopeful or afraid of 2004. I cannot literally run ahead or stretch into 2004; and as we saw, it is a literal running ahead that is needed for Heidegger's purpose of 'interiorizing' death.[1] If I will in fact die ten years after these words are written, I *cannot* literally run ahead,

---

1. It is equally necessary for the 'solution' of Heidegger's 'wholeness' problem, which I have had to neglect in this study. I should add that not all of Heidegger's notions about time are absurd. He has one interesting point, which he himself states with extreme obscurity but which has been restated in more accessible language by C. M. Sherover in *Heidegger, Kant and Time* (Bloomington: Indiana University Press, 1971), especially pp. 191 ff. and 260 ff.

stretch out, and catch up with my death. In any nonperverse sense it is *not* true that I am my end while I am alive; and more generally it is not true that I am already all my not-yets. No amount of verbal juggling will make it otherwise.

DEATH AS OUR 'CAPITAL POSSIBILITY'

Ferrater Mora, a Spanish admirer of Heidegger, has referred to Heidegger's view that 'the being of Dasein is a being unto death' as a 'famous contention.'[1] In the light of our remarks in the preceding section it may be questioned whether the statements Heidegger makes in this connection qualify as a 'contention,' but it is probably true that, of all the many phrases he has coined, none has been picked up by more people than '*Sein zum Tode*'. However, both he and several of his disciples regard another of his 'contentions' as the real climax of his investigation into the nature of death. This is his repeated assertion that death is a 'possibility'—possibility as opposed to actuality. Most people, we are given to understand, have an incorrect attitude towards death because they regard it as an actuality, because in various ways they try to 'weaken' its possibility. Heidegger, on the other hand, as a result of his great insight that death is a possibility and not an actuality, has shown 'the correct attitude of man towards death.' These are the words of William A. Luijpen, a Dutch enthusiast, who proceeds to claim—something Heidegger himself also asserts—that in characterizing death as a possibility, Heidegger has 'unveiled' the 'true meaning of death.'[2] In this and the next section I will try to explain and evaluate these claims as well as some of the related pronouncements of certain of Heidegger's followers.

Throughout *Being and Time* Heidegger speaks of death as a possibility. It is our uttermost, our unoutstrippable or unsurpassable, our ownmost and our nonrelational possibility. It would be unfair to say that Heidegger never explains what he means when he describes death as a 'possibility.' After speaking in this way for some twenty-five pages, close to

---

1. José Ferrater Mora, *Being and Death* (Berkeley and Los Angeles: University of California Press, 1965), p. 117.
2. William A. Luijpen, *Existential Phenomenology*, rev. ed. (Pittsburgh: Duquesne University Press, 1969), p. 393.

the end of the chapter on death, he finally explains what he means; and it turns out that he means neither what the word means in any of its ordinary senses *nor* what he himself had meant by it throughout *BT*. The new use, it turns out, is *utterly and totally* different from all these other uses.

Something must be said at this stage about the special sense of 'possibility' Heidegger had introduced earlier in *BT*, in which he uses the word throughout the book *except* when talking about death. Dasein, Heidegger writes, 'determines its own character as the kind of entity it is, and it does so in every case in terms of a possibility which it itself *is* and which it understands' (pp. 303–304, Heidegger's italics). 'Possibility' in this sense is to be 'sharply distinguished both from empty logical possibility and from the contingency of something present-at-hand' (p. 183). Evidently Heidegger uses 'possibility' to refer to the alternatives which we can choose or, more precisely, which we *know* ourselves to be capable of choosing. 'Dasein is such that in every case it has understood . . . that it is to be thus or thus. As such understanding it "knows" *what* it is capable of' (p. 184, Heidegger's italics), where the 'knowing' is of a nontheoretical kind. None of this is terribly clear and, as usual, not a single illustration is provided. However, one can in a general way see what Heidegger has in mind. Macquarrie has in several places explained what this sense of 'possibility' comes to. Thus, in a glossary appended to his book *Martin Heidegger*, he writes: 'Possibility, in Heidegger's thought, does not mean just any contingency that may happen, but refers to the open future for which the Dasein can decide.'[1] In another book, also largely devoted to Heidegger, he emphasizes that 'by possibility Heidegger does not mean simply a contingency that might happen to me, but a genuine possibility of existence which man may in a certain way choose for himself.'[2] Similarly, Demske explains that 'in Heidegger's existential phenomenology possibility indicates what Dasein can be, do or become.'[3] 'Possibility' here clearly refers to an action or a strategy or a mode of life (something like Sartre's 'fundamental project') which a human being may adopt or choose. Heroism or cowardice, I believe, would be examples of a person's or at least of some people's possibilities in this sense. I add the qualification 'some people's' because Heidegger is very emphatic that the freedom of

---

1. John Macquarrie, *Martin Heidegger* (Richmond, VA: John Knox Press, 1968), p. 62.
2. *ET*, p. 119.
3. *BMT*, p. 20.

choice he favors is not to be confused with 'a free-floating potentiality-for-Being in the sense of "liberty" or "indifference"' (p. 183). Human beings know themselves to be able to choose between *certain* alternatives, but 'thrownness' restricts the range of what in a given situation is possible.

Now, when Heidegger maintains that death is a person's possibility, he is *not* using 'possibility' in the sense just explained. It appears that Heidegger has been misunderstood in this connection not only by Sartre, who is here writing in opposition to Heidegger, but also by his devoted followers. Not noticing Heidegger's shift from the sense of 'possibility' explained in the preceding paragraph to the totally different sense I have yet to explain, they have delivered some altogether startling pronouncements, which, as it ultimately turns out, are not at all implied in Heidegger's doctrine that death is a possibility. I have in mind here what may be called the 'golden opportunity' view of death and the even more amazing notion that death is the 'crown' of our lives. Heidegger repeatedly refers to death as our *ausgezeichnete Möglichkeit*, which M-R translate, weakly and inaccurately, as 'our distinctive possibility' and for which a more accurate translation would be 'splendid' or 'distinguished possibility'.[1] This and similar statements have apparently been taken to mean that death is something like our golden opportunity. Glenn Gray speaks of death as 'life's greatest possibility' as well as our 'great privilege and challenge' which is something to be 'welcomed.'[2] Luijpen, after remarking correctly, though not very originally, that human life would not be 'what it is without death,' proceeds to affirm that 'death is the mode of potential being which is most proper to man'; it is nothing less, in fact, than 'the most proper possibility of his existence.'[3] Not to be outdone, Macquarrie calls it our 'capital possibility.'[4] These expressions suggest

---

1. *Ausgezeichnet* is a perfectly common German word meaning 'splendid', 'excellent', 'outstanding', 'distinguished', 'first-class'. When I went to high school in Vienna, the highest grade for a course, corresponding to the A of American schools, was *ausgezeichnet*. It is used only as a term of praise; and if Heidegger meant anything less than 'splendid' or 'excellent possibility', he certainly picked a most unfortunate word. Even if, in fact, he means nothing more than what is meant by the English 'distinctive' (which itself is far from clear in this context), the word *ausgezeichnet* will continue to have the old associations for most readers.

2. PD, pp. 54, 61.

3. Luijpen, *Existential Phenomenology*, pp. 390–91. Luijpen also characterizes death as the 'highest instance' (whatever this means) of man's being-in-the-world (p. 398).

4. John Macquarrie, *Studies in Christian Existentialism* (London: SCM Press, 1966), p. 55. Hereafter cited as *SCE*.

that death is like the opportunity that comes to an understudy for a great singer when the latter is suddenly taken ill. Lotte Lehmann had her great opportunity, her 'capital possibility,' when the renowned Marie Gutheil-Schoder could not sing the role of the Composer in the Vienna premiere of *Ariadne auf Naxos*. Father Demske, after telling us that death is 'the possibility of all possibilities,' finally reaches the remarkable conclusion that it is the 'crown and culmination of human life.'[1] Using almost the same language, the German writer Paul Hühnerfeld concludes that 'death becomes the crowning [*die Krönung*] of . . . life.'[2] I do not think I over-stated the case when I referred to such pronouncements as startling. Except when bent on suicide or in the midst of terrible suffering, we do *not* normally regard death as something wonderful that is to be welcomed but, on the contrary, as something to be avoided and put off as long as possible. I believe that the conductor of the Vienna premiere of *Ariadne auf Naxos* was Franz Schalk, a sane and kindly man, who took a fatherly interest in Lotte Lehmann. I cannot imagine him saying to her, even in jest, 'Lottchen—your greatest opportunity has come. If you were still alive tomorrow, you could sing the Composer in place of Gutheil-Schoder. However, you will be dead before the day is up—this is your capital possibility.' Wild and Schrag do not speak of death as 'the crown and culmination of our lives,' but it appears that they, too, are guided by Heidegger's initial use of 'possibility' when they declare that death is a 'task' or an 'act.' Death, writes Schrag, is 'not simply a contingent hap-pening,' it is 'a task or an existential project.'[3] Rightly conceived, death becomes a task or a responsibility which Dasein must assume.[4] In a sim-ilar vein Wild declares that death 'is an *actual act* to be lived through by an individual alone.'[5]

---

1. *BMD*, p. 25.

2. Paul Hühnerfeld, *In Sachen Heidegger* (Munich, 1961), p. 78. In the passage from which I quote Hühnerfeld states and endorses what he takes to be Heidegger's message. It should be added that Hühnerfeld's book is not another string of paraphrases and panegyrics masquerading as a com-mentary on Heidegger's philosophy. On the contrary, it is a book of much interest, containing more biographical material about Heidegger than any other source I know. Hühnerfeld did not at all admire Heidegger's character, and he regarded his influence as in many ways unwholesome. This critical judgment did not, however, extend to Heidegger's philosophy. It is regrettable that, as the result of a car accident, Hühnerfeld attained the 'crown' of his life at the early age of thirty-four.

3. *EF*, p. 108.

4. Ibid.

5. *CE*, p. 83, my italics.

It will be of some interest to evaluate these 'opportunity', 'crown', and 'task' notions of death before we follow Heidegger into his explanation of what he does mean by speaking of death as a possibility. To this end it will be helpful to distinguish between what I will call (a) deadness, (b) the death-moment, (c) death-producing events, and (d) dying. First of all, a few words about the distinction between (a) and (b). By 'death-moment' I shall mean the first moment following the conclusion of a person's life. A doctor may report that his patient, Samuel Blau, died at 5:04 on Monday, January 11, 2002. This would be Samuel Blau's death-moment. From then on, for all eternity, he will be dead. This fact, which can be truly asserted of Samuel Blau, is what I will mean by his 'deadness'. It is tempting, but also very misleading, to speak of Samuel Blau's 'state' of deadness, and I am deliberately avoiding such language (I will return to this point in the next section). By 'death-producing event' I shall mean the kind of thing that would be mentioned as the cause of death in a newspaper obituary or in a biography—for example, cancer, a heart attack, suicide, a plane crash, being run over by a car, and so on. Such an account frequently differs from a detailed medical report which would list the *immediate* physiological antecedents as cause of death. I am using the word 'event' in a very broad sense here so that it would include both actions and conditions which are not normally described as actions. Suicide would be an example of an action which is a death-producing event and so would a dangerous attempt to rescue somebody from a fire. Cancer, heart attacks, or being assassinated are death-producing events which we do not normally regard as actions. My use of 'death-producing event' is not at all precise, but for our limited purpose no further explanation is necessary. Finally, by 'dying' I will mean the phase in the life of an individual between the beginning of the death-producing event and his death-moment. In the case of a person who is killed in a plane crash this would be a very short period. In the case of somebody dying of a disease like cancer it could be an extended period. I believe that this roughly coincides with the everyday use of the word. Like the latter, it is far from precise, but again this will not affect any of the issues in our subsequent discussion.

Let us now return to what I called the golden opportunity—and the crown—notions of death and let us concentrate on Demske's statement that death is the 'crown and culmination' of human life. It should be noted that Demske is asserting this of *every* human life. It should also be remembered that, although he is a believer in immortality, Father Demske is not in this context referring to survival of any kind. He is expounding and defending the views of Heidegger. Now, it is not false but *meaningless* to speak either of deadness or the death-moment as the 'crown and culmination' of a human life. In any intelligible sense, the culmination of a person's life must be an event or sequence of events *in* his life. It must be something occurring while he is alive. It makes sense and it is probably true that the crown and culmination of Winston Churchill's life was his leadership of Great Britain during the war against Hitler, but it makes no sense to say that the crown and culmination of his life was his death-moment on a certain day in January 1965 or his deadness since that time. It is not meaningless to speak of the death-producing event in a person's life or of his dying as crown and culmination. Such a statement is not meaningless but, asserted as a universal proposition, it is quite certainly false. In Rossellini's *Il general della rovere*, the main character, Bardone, is a small-time crook in an Italian town who is mistaken for the leader of the Resistance against the Fascists. He courageously goes to his death when he could have escaped such a fate by revealing his true identity. It may well be true that his refusal to save himself *was* the crown of his life. Again, some people whose lives were undistinguished by any high-minded deeds showed remarkable courage and equanimity during their terminal illness. There is a moving illustration of this in *Der Tod des Kleinbürgers* by the Austrian poet and novelist Franz Werfel. The story is about the last days of Karl Fiala, a retired janitor, who lost his modest savings in the inflation that followed the First World War. Fiala has an epileptic son who is unable to hold a job. His one desire is to make sure that after his death the son should not be committed to a mental institution. He has taken out life insurance which would adequately provide for his widow and son, but the premiums are conditional on Fiala's not dying until he reaches the age of sixty-five. Two months before his sixty-fifth birthday he becomes mortally ill and is moved to a hospital room reserved for patients who are expected to die within a matter of hours. Against all predictions and to the annoyance of the doctors and nurses he refuses to die and exceeds his goal by two days. Throughout the last two days he is heard to mumble, 'Es ist vollbracht' (It is accomplished). Fiala had been a meek and humble man, completely dominated by his wife and her sister.

His final struggle was the only heroic episode in his life. It is arguable that in such a case the individual's dying is indeed the crown of his life. However, as a universal proposition, Demske's statement is surely untenable. Clarence Darrow's life had many highlights, but there was nothing at all interesting about his life during his final illness. Similarly, Winston Churchill died of complications from a fall, after several years of physical and mental decline. When Father Demske claims that death is the crown and culmination of human life, he is not, it seems clear, intending to assert the false but intelligible proposition that either the death-producing event or the person's dying is the climax of every human life. He is speaking of deadness just as, as we shall see, Heidegger is speaking of deadness when he declares death to be a possibility. Father Demske is speaking of deadness; and hence his pronouncement is not intelligible and false but nonsense. Similar remarks apply to the golden-opportunity statements and the statements that death is a task or an act. It is nonsense to speak of deadness or death-moments as acts or tasks; and it will also in most contexts be absurd to speak of them as 'capital possibilities.' It is not necessarily nonsense and it may in certain cases be true that a death-producing event is a task and a capital possibility; and the same holds for 'dying'. As universal propositions, however, these statements are quite certainly false.

THE 'POSSIBILITY' OF THE IMPOSSIBILITY OF EXISTING

Let us now return to Heidegger himself. The chapter on death in *BT* consists of eight sections. After having told us throughout the preceding sections that death is a 'possibility,' Heidegger finally realizes in the last section that his use of the word in this context may be easily misunderstood. Before telling us what he does mean he discusses in some detail three possible misunderstandings. First Heidegger notes that his statement that 'Being-towards-death is Being-towards-a-possibility' may suggest that he is thinking of death as a possibility which can and perhaps should be 'actualized' the way in which we might actualize a possible visit to the opera or a possible trip to Paris. Heidegger is emphatic that in calling death Dasein's 'possibility' he does not use the word in this way and, furthermore, that the attitude he recommends towards death is in no way like our attitude towards a possibility which we are trying to actualize. The latter attitude, which he calls 'concernfully Being out for something possible' has 'a tendency to *annihilate the possibility* of the possible by making it available to us' (p. 305, Heidegger's italics). Such an attitude 'weakens' the possibility of death, and Heidegger is concerned to do the opposite. In any event, if he meant by 'possibility' something that we can actualize he would in effect be recommending suicide; and this is not what he is doing: 'To concern oneself with actualizing what is thus possible would have to signify, "bringing about one's demise." But if this were done, Dasein would deprive itself of the very ground for an existing Being-towards-death.'[1]

In his discussion of the two other misunderstandings, Heidegger does not mention any further senses of 'possibility', but instead he mentions two attitudes towards death which he may be taken to recommend and which he is in fact eager to disavow. The first of these is 'brooding' (*grübeln*). In brooding 'one "thinks about death," pondering over when and how this possibility may perhaps be actualized' (p. 305). It is true that brooding does not 'fully take away' from death 'its character as a possibility.' However, just as we weaken the possibility of the possible when we are trying to actualize it, so brooding, too, 'weakens' the possibility of death by 'calculating how we are to have it at our disposal' (pp. 305–306). In this way death 'is to show as little as possible of its possibility' (p. 306). To achieve an authentic being-towards-death we must do the exact opposite: 'Death must be understood *as a possibility*, it must be cultivated as a possibility, and we must *endure it as a possibility* in the way we comport ourselves toward it' (ibid., G p. 261, Heidegger's italics). Nor is *erwarten* (what M-R translate as 'expecting') the right attitude; and again for the same reason: 'To expect something possible is always to under-

---

1. Macquarrie is the only Heideggerian who shows any awareness that Heidegger is using the word 'possibility' in a strange way here. He admits (*SCE*, p. 54) that it is 'very odd to talk of death as a possibility at all' and, like Heidegger, he finds it necessary to explain that Heidegger is not asking us to 'rush suicidally into death' (ibid.). However, Macquarrie shows not the slightest awareness that there has been a shift in Heidegger's use of 'possibility' and that the word in this context does not mean what it had meant throughout *BT*. Gelven discusses at some length what he calls Heidegger's 'principle that possibility is prior to actuality.' This principle, he tells us, is 'rampant in Heidegger's thought' (*CBT*, p. 75), but it does not once occur to him that when Heidegger contrasts possibility with actuality in connection with death, we are no longer presented with the principle that had been 'rampant' in the earlier chapters.

stand it and to "have" it with regard to whether and when and how it will be actually present-at-hand' (ibid.). If anything, it seems, expecting is worse than brooding as far as weakening or falsifying the possibility of death is concerned. Expecting, Heidegger tells us quite plausibly, 'is essentially a *waiting for . . . actualization*' (ibid., Heidegger's italics). In expecting, he adds, 'one leaps away from the possible and gets a foothold on the actual . . . by the very nature of expecting, the possible is drawn into the actual, arising out of the actual and returning to it' (ibid.).

At this stage the reader may despair of ever discovering what Heidegger means when he speaks of death as 'possibility' and what attitude, different from trying to bring about death, brooding over death, or expecting death, he champions. All possibilities, if I may revert to one of the ordinary senses of the word, seem to have been exhausted.[1] Not so. The right attitude and the clue to the 'true nature' of the possibility of death is 'vorlaufen in die Möglichkeit,' which M-R misleadingly translate as 'anticipation of the possibility' and which I shall translate very literally as 'running ahead into the possibility'. We already met *vorlaufen* or 'running ahead', in section 3 in connection with Heidegger's view that the future can be transported into the present. At first sight 'running ahead' may not seem significantly different from 'expecting', but Heidegger tells us that it involves an 'understanding' that is absent in expecting. In the kind of 'coming close' that is represented by 'running ahead,' one comes closer to death 'understandingly.' This does *not* 'tend towards making available something actual' (p. 306). On the contrary, 'as one comes closer understandingly, the possibility of the possible just becomes "greater." *The closest closeness which one may have in Being towards death as a possibility, is as far as possible from anything actual*' (pp. 306–307, Heidegger's italics). We have now arrived at the answer to the riddle. In this 'closest closeness' the nature of the possibility becomes 'unveiled.' The 'understanding penetrates into it' and reveals it '*as the possibility of the impossibility of any existence at all*' (p. 307, Heidegger's

---

1. Gelven is much impressed by this feature of Heidegger's presentation. 'His style,' Gelven observes, 'is almost that of the mystery-story writer—by making the mystery seem so insoluble, the success of the brilliant detective is all the more admired.' Gelven adds that 'this is a legitimate part of Heidegger's charm as a great teacher' (*CBT*, p. 146). Gelven's book consists mostly of repetitions of Heideggerian formulations in the obscure language of the original, followed by little cries of love such as 'brilliant', 'acute', and 'even more acute'. I am indebted to him for the discovery that 'in spite of its rather frequent occurrence death comes only once for each person' (p. 142).

italics). In a later chapter this 'possibility of the impossibility of existence' is identified with the 'schlechthinnige Nichtigkeit' of Dasein, which M-R translate as its 'utter nullity' and which might perhaps be more idiomatically rendered as 'total nothingness' (p. 354, G p. 306). The unveiling reveals death as 'the possibility of the impossibility of *every* way of comporting oneself towards anything, of *every* way of existing' (p. 307, my italics). 'As we "run ahead into the possibility," it "becomes 'ever greater,' that is to say, the possibility reveals itself to be 'such that it knows no measure at all, no more or less, but signifies the possibility of the measureless impossibility of existence'"' (p. 307, G p. 262).

It now becomes clear why Heidegger is so intent on using the word 'possibility'. Death is not an 'actuality', not a state, but the absence of all states. Death is a possibility because it 'gives Dasein nothing to be "actualized," nothing which Dasein, as actual, could itself *be*' (ibid., Heidegger's italics). If we regard death as a possibility we will not make the mistake of 'picturing' (the word Heidegger uses is *ausmalen*, which literally means 'paint a content') it as an actuality.

What are we to say of this conclusion and the way in which Heidegger arrived at it? Primarily two things—first, if one agrees, as I do, that there is no survival, Heidegger is quite right in describing death as a *total* absence, and, second, that his use of the word 'possibility' is fantastically misleading. Surely speaking of death as 'possibility' when what and *all* that is meant is that death is the total *absence* of experiences and behavior, the annihilation of all consciousness, the impossibility of every way of comporting oneself, is carrying the misuse of language to the ultimate degree. The total absence of experiences and behavior is most emphatically *not* what we mean by 'possibility' in any of its ordinary senses, and it is *equally* not what Heidegger himself meant when he introduced the word 'possibility' in his special sense to mean the actions or conduct or mode of life which a person may choose. No wonder that he has been misunderstood by his own followers, and no wonder that his pronouncement sounds strange and is regarded by his uncritical worshipers not simply as a statement of the unbeliever's view on the subject of survival but as a remarkable and profound insight. If Heidegger had, from the start, used the proper language and simply spoken of death as total annihilation, there would have been no occasion for all the hocus-pocus about the 'closest closeness' to the 'possibility of the possible' which becomes 'ever greater.' Equally, there would have been no occasion for posturing as a great discoverer who 'unveils' and 'understandingly penetrates' the nature of death. Instead, Heidegger might have given us the reasons—and there are very good ones—for supposing that death is really the end and that belief in survival is an illusion. Bertrand Russell reached the same result with less effort and without fear of being misunderstood in his essay 'What I Believe,' in which he wrote, quite simply, 'I believe that when I die I shall rot, and nothing of my ego will survive.'[1]

When Heidegger talks about the 'possibility of the impossibility of every way of existing,' the word 'possibility' is altogether superfluous. What makes death a 'non-actuality' and thus a 'possibility' in his strange special sense *is* the impossibility of every way of existing. This is what the possibility in the new sense *consists in*. The redundancy of 'possibility' in the phrase 'possibility of the impossibility of existing' is not at once apparent because the reader is apt to revert to the familiar sense in which 'possibility' is contrasted with probability or certainty. It is 'possible' but not certain that I will die five years from now. Heidegger is very definitely not using 'possible' in *this* sense when characterizing death as a possibility. For Heidegger repeatedly insists—quite rightly, though not very originally—that death is a *certainty* and not just a possibility in *this* sense. However, the existence and familiarity of this ordinary sense tends to hide the redundancy of 'possibility' in Heidegger's phrase 'possibility of the impossibility of every way of existing.' 'Possibility' adds nothing here, or, rather, nothing but confusion.

If we ignore his continued employment of the word 'possibility' even after it has become clear that he means nothing of the kind, Heidegger's final formulation is not without merit. If one grants that there is no survival, then it is well to emphasize that death is an *utter* or *total* or *radical* absence. Our everyday language and the writings of poets are studded with images that make us, even those who are unbelievers, on occasion think of death as a form of rest or sleep or peace—a shadowy, low-grade form of consciousness. We, or some of us, have a tendency, as Heidegger puts it, to 'paint a content' into our notion of death. In opposition to this tendency, it is well to emphasize that, if survival is a myth, death is not a form of rest

---

1. Bertrand Russell, 'What I Believe,' in *Why I Am Not a Christian* (New York: Simon and Schuster, 1957), p. 54; (London: Allen and Unwin, 1957), p. 43.

or sleep, that it is not a low-grade form of consciousness, but the absence of all consciousness. Heidegger is right to speak of death as '*measureless* impossibility of existence.' It is not just a partial absence like blindness or deafness or the loss of one's singing voice or paralysis in one part of one's body. It is the total absence of capacities and experiences. It is, as Heidegger puts it, the 'impossibility of *every* way of comporting oneself towards anything, of *every* way of existing.' There are grounds for saying that, at least for most people, blindness would be worse than deafness, that losing one's capacity to sing is not as terrible as becoming paralyzed from the neck down. These losses are not 'measureless'; they are losses experienced by living individuals and involve states which can be compared. We cannot in the same way compare the absence of all states with any given state. In this sense we may agree that death is 'measureless.'

It will be helpful in some of our later discussions if I offer a slightly different formulation of what is sound in Heidegger's conclusion that death is 'the possibility of the impossibility of every way of existing.' Following Aristotle, several recent writers have distinguished between 'actions' and 'passions'. An 'action' in this sense is anything a person does, for example, delivering a speech, playing a game of tennis, singing a song, calling an ambulance. A 'passion' is anything which happens to a human being—the joy he feels when listening to beautiful music, the boredom he experiences when listening to a tedious lecture, or the pain he endures after suffering an accident. This distinction is not of course very precise, but it is one which all of us make in certain situations. Now, when people describe death as rest or sleep or peace, they have realized that death is not an 'action', but, to the extent to which they are serious, they mistakenly regard it as a 'passion'— presumably the most passive of all passions. However, if it is granted that there is no afterlife, then death, just like nonexistence before birth, is neither an action nor a passion. If we introduce the word 'state' to mean any action or passion, we can express our (and Heidegger's) point by saying that, unlike rest, sleep, and peace, death is not a state.[1]

Readers of *BT* will be familiar with the fact that Heidegger never says anything simply and clearly if he can say it oddly, obscurely, and ponderously; and I have no doubt that the desire to sound esoteric and original is part of the reason for his fantastic misuse of the word 'possibility'.

---

1. For a fuller discussion of this point see my article ED, pp. 482 ff.

There is also, however, a logical fallacy behind it. Heidegger evidently believes that if something that can be meaningfully talked about is not an 'actuality' in the sense in which he is here using the word, then it must be a possibility. Death is not an actuality; hence it is a 'possibility'. This argument, which hovers in the background of Heidegger's discussion, calls for two comments. In the first place, the word 'actuality' is ambiguous. There is a sense in which Heidegger is right to deny that death is something actual, but there is another and perfectly natural sense in which it is (or becomes) an actuality. Jefferson and President Kennedy, to take two familiar cases, are actually dead. It is *a fact* that they are dead. Their death has *actually* occurred. My own death has not yet occurred but at some time in the future it will occur, and when it occurs it will be an actuality. Let us call this the 'occurrence' sense of 'actuality', or 'actuality$_o$'. I already explained what Heidegger means when he says that death is not an actuality. He does not deny that it actually occurs. He means that it is a total absence, that it does not have any 'positive content' which can be 'pictured,' that it is not a 'state' in the sense described in the last paragraph. Let us call this the state or content-sense of 'actuality', or 'actuality$_s$'. Now, Heidegger argues that since death is not an actuality in this latter sense, since it is not an actuality$_s$ it must therefore be a possibility. This conclusion would follow if it were true that whatever can be meaningfully talked about must either be an actuality$_s$ or a possibility; but this last proposition is an incomplete disjunction. It is most emphatically not true, and we have just seen that it is not true. Death is not an actuality$_s$, and the same is true of our nonexistence before birth. Death and nonexistence before birth are neither actualities$_s$ nor possibilities. They are total absences. The statement that anything which is not an actuality$_s$ must be a possibility can only be rescued by a redefinition of 'possibility' which in this instance is entirely arbitrary and perverse; and this is of course precisely what Heidegger has done.

It should be added that Heidegger is extremely unfair to those whom he describes as 'brooding about' and to those who are said to 'expect' death. I do not suppose that the 'brooders' and the 'expecters' are any more or less clear-headed in their thoughts about death than the rest of mankind (confining ourselves to all who do not seriously believe in survival). If so, then at times they probably vaguely think of death as a low-grade kind of consciousness; and to the extent to which they do this, they are in need of correction. However, at other times they realize only too well that death is a total absence, and they presumably justify their gloom either because they have not enjoyed life and will, long before they would like this to happen, be deprived of any opportunities to make up for their previous lack of enjoyment, or because they have enjoyed and are enjoying life, but will, sooner or later, be utter 'nullities' such that any continuation of their enjoyments will be impossible. When the brooders and the expecters regard death as an actuality, they almost certainly mean (most of the time at least) what is entirely true and what Heidegger does not dispute, namely, that they, like other human beings, will die, i.e., that their death will become an actuality$_o$.

Various of his disciples have claimed that Heidegger is to be credited with a major discovery in distinguishing 'running ahead into the possibility' from mere 'expecting'. The realization that *vorlaufen* is 'quite different' from mere *erwarten*, Gelven tells us, fills 'the mind with great enlightenment.'[1] Schrag speaks of *vorlaufen* as the 'activity' of 'anticipatory appropriation' without which we cannot 'authentically understand death.'[2] In the course of this 'anticipatory appropriation' death is 'existentially preenacted.'[3] Heideggerians like Gelven and Schrag, whose minds are filled with 'the great enlightenment' provided by Heidegger's notion of running ahead into the possibility, 'existentially preeenact' their death. Others less fortunate are condemned to an inauthentic life in which they merely expect death. It is suggested that it is possible to preenact death in a way that would correspond to our ability to *re*enact past events. However, since our anticipatory acts, whatever they may be, will always be 'states' in the sense explained earlier and since death is a total absence, a preenactment of death is impossible. I can commit suicide or live dangerously, thereby courting an early death; but this would be '*en*actment' and not a 'preenactment' of death. I can start sleeping in a (suitably ventilated) coffin, and I can simulate death; but none of this will be a 'preenactment' of death analogous to the 'reenactment' of past events. If 'existential preenactment of death' is not to be a senseless expression, it can mean no more than realizing that one is going to die and that death is total annihilation and not a

---

1. *CBT*, p. 155. Although 'translations cannot carry the full subtlety of the meaning,' it is reassuring to know that one need not be a 'native German' to be receptive to this enlightenment.

2. *EF*, p. 115.

3. Ibid., p. 113.

low-grade form of consciousness; and this is a feat which has been quite commonly accomplished without assistance from Heidegger.

I referred in passing to the fact that Sartre is one of those who have misunderstood what Heidegger means when he describes death as a possibility. Sartre thinks Heidegger is clearly wrong. Referring to death, he writes, 'this perpetual appearance of chance at the heart of my projects cannot be apprehended as *my* possibility but, on the contrary, as the nihilation of all my possibilities, a nihilation which *itself is no longer a part of my possibilities*. Thus death is not my possibility of no longer realizing a presence in the world but rather an *always possible nihilation of my possibles which is outside my possibilities*.'[1] Sartre is right to object to Heidegger, but he objects for the wrong reasons. When Heidegger finally explains what he means in this context by 'possibility', it becomes clear that he is really saying just what Sartre is saying and what Russell is saying and what I am saying, namely, that death amounts to total extinction. Heidegger is *not wrong* but *perverse*. He uses language which is almost certain to be misunderstood, and the misuse, as I have indicated, is not completely unintentional.

LIVING DYING AND DEAD DYING

It should be noted that Heideggerians constantly do precisely what is impermissible if we are to be guided by Heidegger's explanation of what he opposes in calling death a possibility. They constantly 'reify' death, i.e., they regard it as an 'actuality' in the objectionable sense of the term. We already saw how Father Demske's enthusiasm led him to the remarkable conclusion that death is the crown and culmination of human life and how Wild and Schrag came to speak of it as a task and act. Similar reifications, but not so explicitly, are indulged in by numerous Heideggerians and by Heidegger himself when they point to the 'methodological difficulties' which one encounters in dealing with the question 'What is death?' Father Boros has been much concerned with these problems. 'Philosophical reflections on death,' he observes, 'seem to have no point since we have no direct experience of death.'[2] Perhaps, Boros suggests, we can get

---

1. Jean-Paul Sartre, *Being and Nothingness* (New York: Philosophical Library, 1956), p. 537, Sartre's italics.
2. *MT*, p. 1.

around this difficulty by watching other people die. Unfortunately, this will not solve the problem. For 'as we watch at somebody's death-bed' what we witness 'is assuredly not death *in its inner reality*; it is only the outward aspect of death.'[1] Boros then inquires whether we might not 'receive a decisive, revealing answer from people who have been near death, or have been given up for dead by those about them.' Such an inquiry, alas, will also fail to answer our questions, since people who were close to death did not really experience *death* as distinct from *closeness* to death.

Macquarrie has gone into great detail about these seemingly insuperable difficulties. In an essay titled 'Death and Its Significance,' in which he commends Heidegger's teachings to his fellow-Christians as 'a sound and contemporary basis on which to rear' their 'theological superstructure,'[2] Macquarrie is concerned to explore what he calls the 'ontological' or 'existential' character of death. How, he asks, can a person 'understand' his 'own death'? Macquarrie has been greatly impressed by the 'phenomenological method' as employed by Heidegger in his 'existential analytic.' By using this method Heidegger has succeeded in throwing much light on such 'structures' as 'understanding, moods, speech, anxiety, concern and solicitude.' These structures can be phenomenologically explored in our living through them, but our death is something 'which we do *not* live through.'[3] If so, how can death be 'investigated phenomenologically' and, what is apparently the same thing, how could we achieve an 'existential understanding' of death? The situation of the ontological explorer seems quite desperate: 'Anyone who undergoes death seems by that very fact to be robbed of any possibility of understanding and analyzing what it was to undergo death. He has ceased to be, therefore he has ceased to be disclosed to himself; his being is no longer lit up to himself in the only way that would seem to make anything like an existential analysis possible, and so it appears that he cannot by any means understand what the undergoing of death may be like, as an existential phenomenon.[4] In another work Macquarrie has succinctly described the plight of the phenomenological investigator who has died: 'He has ceased to be. . . . Therefore he has ceased to be disclosed to himself, and has no possibility of understanding what his death has been.'[5] In his despair, Mac-

---

1. *MT*, p. 1, my italics.
2. *SCE*, p. 57.
3. Ibid., Macquarrie's italics.
4. Ibid.
5. *ET*, p. 117.

quarrie, like Boros, raises the question whether relevant 'information may be obtained' by studying the death of other people. At first sight this appears a promising possibility. For, in the case of other people who die before we do, we 'can see them ceasing to exist, going out of the world, so to speak.'[1] Further reflection, however, shows that studying the death of others will not get us out of our predicament. There are two devastating objections to anybody who thinks otherwise. In the first place, such a study yields no more than 'a vicarious experience of death.' When we study the death of others what we are experiencing is the loss sustained by the survivors, 'but what is really of interest to us is the *loss of being sustained by the deceased himself*, and this remains completely inaccessible to us.'[2] Moreover, as already observed, the deceased, being deceased, cannot attend to his deadness—he cannot experience his loss of being; and, even if he could, he would be unable to tell the living what this loss of being is like. He can no 'longer communicate with us to describe that loss of being.'[3]

Boros and Macquarrie have in effect reified death in exactly the way Heidegger regards as impermissible when he (unfairly) denounces the brooders and expecters and when he tells us that death is not an actuality. The 'inner reality' of the dead person's death and the 'loss of being sustained by the deceased himself,' which he finds impossible to describe to us, are treated as dark and mysterious states whose nature we would like to discover but which, for the reasons indicated, we find extremely difficult to explore. This 'inquiry,' it must now be added, is by no means an accidental aberration on the part of two Heideggerian enthusiasts. It is found in many other Heideggerians and in Heidegger himself.[4] We would like to 'grasp,' writes Heidegger, 'the way-to-be' referred to as 'coming-to-an-end.' We are 'asking about the ontological meaning of the dying of

---

1. *SCE*, p. 52; *ET*, p. 117.
2. *SCE*, p. 52, my italics.
3. *ET*, p. 118.
4. José Ferrater Mora is another philosopher who is seriously concerned to explore the inner nature of the death of the deceased. In *Being and Death*, pp. 175–76, he states the predicament of anybody engaging in such an investigation: 'We can "see" that people die; we can think of our own death as an event which will take place sooner or later, but we do not seem to be able to experience death in the same way as we do other "events" such as pleasure, pain, good health, illness, senility. All we can "see" of death is its "residue," for example, a corpse.' It should be noted that a dead person is here automatically regarded as more than a corpse. For a detailed critique of the grotesque confusions in Mora's answer to this problem—especially the notion that a survivor can 'share' the dead person's death—see my article ED, pp. 480–81, 487–91.

the person who dies' (*BT*, p. 283). Just like Boros and Macquarrie, Heidegger first points out that nobody can experience his own death: 'When Dasein reaches its wholeness in death, it simultaneously loses the Being of its "there." By its transition to no-longer-Dasein, it gets lifted right out of the possibility of experiencing this transition and of understanding it as something experienced. Surely this sort of thing is denied to any particular Dasein in relation to itself' (*BT*, p. 281). Heidegger then turns to the question of the death of other people and, like Boros and Macquarrie, he concludes that it is of no help to us: 'In such Being-with-the-dead, the authentic Being-come-to-an-end of the deceased is precisely the sort of thing which we do *not* experience. Death does indeed reveal itself as a loss, but a loss such as is experienced by those who remain. In suffering this loss, however, we have no way of access to the loss-of-Being as such which the dying man "suffers"' (p. 282, Heidegger's italics). Again, in a later section, we are told that 'a psychology of "dying" gives information about the "living" of the person who is "dying" rather than about *dying itself*' (p. 291, my italics).

In other words, there are two kinds of 'dying'. There is the 'dying' a person experiences before he is dead, what is *usually* called 'dying', and this 'living dying' we *can* study; but there is also the 'dying itself', the dying that occurs after the person is dead, his 'dead dying', which is identical with what I above called deadness. The 'dead or nonliving dying' is the loss of being sustained by the deceased, and *its* nature will not be revealed in our study of the 'living dying' of others. Thus, although Heidegger (rightly in my opinion) insists with great emphasis that death is a total absence and not an actuality$_s$, he also, quite inconsistently, treats death as such an actuality.

It may be noted in passing that Boros, Macquarrie, and Heidegger himself believe that, in spite of their extreme gravity, the methodological problems resulting from our inability to attend to our own deadness can be overcome. 'Modern philosophy has gone far,' writes Father Boros, towards overcoming these difficulties. It will come as no surprise that the 'modern philosophy' referred to by Boros is that expounded by Martin Heidegger in *BT*. This philosophy has shown that 'in every act of existence death is present from the beginning.'[1] Similarly, Macquarrie

---

1. *MT*, p. 8.

observes that 'existence is dying, and death is present to us.'[1] Since it is 'in a sense already in the present,' it is after all 'accessible . . . to the investigation of the existential analytic.'[2] If we recall the distinction explained in section 3 between d_o—death in the ordinary sense—and c_d—our concern about death—it will at once be obvious that 'modern philosophy' has not overcome the methodological difficulties which so greatly perplexed the phenomenological explorers. For what we experience, what is available for phenomenological analysis, what becomes 'transparent' is not death, d_o, but c_d, or thoughts and moods concerning death; and these were always available, even before Heidegger's 'existential' analysis. What was not available for phenomenological exploration prior to Heidegger's interiorization is just as unavailable afterwards.

It is hardly necessary to add that the methodological difficulties themselves are completely spurious. If one misconceives death as the 'inner state' of the dead person whose body is the 'outward aspect' of his death or as the state in which the dead person has sustained the most terrible of all losses, then one is bound to be mystified. One will conclude that such a state is inaccessible to the outside observer, who only perceives the 'living dying' and the 'outward aspect'; and it is of course equally inaccessible to the dead person who, being dead, is unable to attend to his deadness. However, there is no justification for thinking about death in this way. If, in agreement with the Heidegger who speaks of death as an utter nullity, we regard it as simply the total absence of experiences and behavior, the 'methodological difficulties' instantly disappear. My deadness after I have died is no more incomprehensible to me than the fact that I did not exist before I was born or, if you like, before I was conceived. I understand perfectly well what is meant by the statement that I was not yet alive in 1800, although I was not then around to do any phenomenological exploring. Similarly, I do not have to be dead and, as a dead man, engage in phenomenological investigations in order to understand *now*, while I am alive, that I will be dead in the year 2100.

---

1. *SCE*, p. 51.
2. Ibid., p. 55.

Four

Death, Anxiety, and the Nothing

T hat Dasein 'has been delivered over to its death,' Heidegger tells us, is not something of which we have 'for the most part . . . explicit or even any theoretical knowledge' (*BT*, p. 295). Our 'thrownness into death reveals itself . . . in a more primordial and impressive manner in . . . anxiety' (ibid.). 'Being-towards-death,' in fact, 'is essentially anxiety' (p. 310). It is essentially 'anxiety' but not 'fear'; and Heidegger is very concerned to distinguish 'anxiety in the face of death' from 'fear in the face of one's demise' (p. 295).[1] The distinction, it appears, is between concern about what we earlier called deadness and fear of what we called the death-producing event.

Anxiety, in the face of death, is 'not an accidental or random mood of "weakness" in some individual' (p. 295). On the contrary, it is 'a basic state-of-mind of Dasein' (ibid.) and, as Heidegger elsewhere assures us, fear itself is only possible because 'anxiety is always latent' (p. 234). In fact 'fear is anxiety, fallen into the "world," inauthentic, and, as such, hidden from itself' (ibid.). The villain in our story, as is usual in Heidegger, is the 'they': 'The "they" concerns itself with transforming this

---

1. I am following M-R in using 'anxiety' for *Angst* and 'fear' for *Furcht*. The translators of 'What Is Metaphysics?' in *Existence and Being* (an exceedingly shoddy and inaccurate translation) render *Angst* as 'dread'. M-R reserve 'dread' for the species of fear to which Heidegger refers as *Grauen* (p. 182, G p. 142).

anxiety into fear in the face of an oncoming event. In addition, the anxiety which has been made ambiguous as fear, is passed off as a weakness with which no self-assured Dasein may have any acquaintance. What is "fitting" according to the unuttered decree of the "they," is indifferent tranquility as to the "fact" that one dies' (p. 298).

The 'they', furthermore, denounces 'thinking about death' as 'a cowardly fear, a sign of insecurity on the part of Dasein, and a somber way of fleeing from the world' (ibid.). According to Heidegger, the reverse is true. It is fear and not anxiety which is 'cowardly.' Inauthentic Dasein 'perverts anxiety into cowardly fear and, in surmounting this fear, only makes known its own cowardliness in the face of anxiety' (p. 311). Moreover, it is true that anxiety tears Dasein away from the world, but this is all to the good. Dasein then can no longer 'understand itself . . . in terms of "the world" and the way things have been publicly interpreted' (p. 232). In this way Dasein is 'thrown back' upon itself and can achieve authenticity.

Anxiety, as we have seen, is the mood or state of mind which gives us our 'primordial' and nontheoretical knowledge that we must die. According to Heidegger, it plays another extremely important role in our proper understanding of death. Heidegger repeatedly emphasizes that, although death is certain, its timing is uncertain. We know that we will die, but we do not know when our death will occur: 'Running ahead brings Dasein face-to-face with a possibility which is constantly certain but which at any moment remains indefinite as to when that possibility will become an impossibility' (p. 356, G p. 308). It scarcely needs to be mentioned that the 'they' once again appears on the scene to do its nefarious work. 'The "they",' we are told, 'covers up what is peculiar in death's certainty—*that it is possible at any moment*' (p. 302, Heidegger's italics). The 'they' evades 'the indefiniteness by conferring definiteness upon it' (ibid.). The 'they' goes about this cover-up in an extremely clever way. It does not 'confer definiteness' upon death by trying to calculate the date of the demise. This kind of definiteness would frighten an inauthentic Dasein too much. It therefore defers death to 'sometime later' and 'interposes' before death 'those urgencies and possibilities which can be taken in at a glance, and which belong to the everyday matters that are closest to us' (p. 302).

Once we have chased away the 'they', we are faced with a serious 'existential' problem. 'Can Dasein,' Heidegger asks, '. . . *understand authentically* its ownmost possibility . . . which is certain and, as such, indefinite?' (p. 304, Heidegger's italics). More specifically: how does 'running ahead', which discloses the indefiniteness of death, accomplish this disclosure? 'How does the running ahead understanding project itself upon a potentiality-for-Being which is certain and which is constantly possible in such a way that the "when" in which the utter impossibility of existence becomes possible remains constantly indefinite?' (p. 310, G p. 265). This is not, Heidegger implies, an idle or trivial question. Quite the reverse: 'In running ahead into the indefinite certainty of death, Dasein opens itself [*öffnet sich*] to a *constant threat* arising out of its own "there"' (ibid., Heidegger's italics).

This 'opening' is an essential part of 'authentic Being-towards-death': 'In this very threat Being-towards-the-end must maintain itself. So little can it tone this down that it must rather cultivate the indefiniteness of the certainty' (ibid.).

But how can this be done? This 'openness' in which we 'must maintain' ourselves and which we 'must cultivate' is something more than a mere theoretical understanding of the fact that the timing of our death is uncertain. 'How,' asks Heidegger, 'is it existentially possible for this constant threat to be genuinely disclosed?' All understanding, he has repeatedly asserted, is accompanied by a mood or state of mind. What is the state of mind which 'genuinely discloses' not just that we must die but that the certainty of death is indefinite? Once again anxiety fills the breach. 'The indefiniteness of death is primordially disclosed in anxiety' (p. 356). Again: '*The state-of-mind which can hold open the utter and constant threat to itself . . . is anxiety*' (p. 310, Heidegger's italics).

It thus appears that two doses of anxiety are in store for an authentic Dasein. It experiences anxiety both when it is face-to-face with its deadness and when it contemplates the indefiniteness of the time of its demise. The latter presumably serves to intensify the anxiety already experienced by the mere contemplation of deadness. Heidegger clearly implies that the greater the anxiety, the more desirable is the experience. It is only in this way that we can explain his recommendation that Dasein should 'cultivate the indefiniteness of the certainty.' This view has not only appealed to Heidegger's disciples. Wolfgang Stegmüller, a German analytic philosopher who is highly critical of certain aspects of Heidegger's thought, nevertheless finds in his work 'a virtually inexhaustible abundance of new . . . insights.'[1] One of these, it appears, is the recommendation just mentioned: 'Authentic Being-towards-death can consist only in the fact that death is not evaded but endured, and indeed precisely in its character as an indeterminate possibility. Such enduring is for Heidegger the ultimate ideal of Existence. . . . Here Dasein first reaches its supreme authenticity.'[2] All of this is reminiscent of Kierkegaard's teaching that 'passion'—not just any passion but 'the tension of inwardness' produced in the person who has faith in the existence of God and the divinity of Jesus in spite of the logical difficulties involved in such beliefs—'is the culmination of existence for an existing individual.'[3]

Before continuing with the account of what Heidegger means by 'anxiety', a further explanation is required of his view on the nature of fear. According to Heidegger fear always has a definite '*wovor*' ('that before which one is or stands'). When we experience fear, we are 'in the face of a detrimental entity within-the-world which comes from some definite region' (p. 230). We are then 'always afraid of this or that definite thing which threatens us in this or that definite way.'[4] If a person has been sentenced to death, what we would, in everyday language, call his 'fear' of the execution would also be called 'fear' by Heidegger. It has an object or a '*wovor*'. Does anxiety have an object? The answer is, yes and no. It does not have an object in the sense of being directed to some particular 'detrimental entity within the world.' However, if saying that it has an object means no more than that it has a direction, then anxiety does have an object. Heidegger offers various accounts of the nature of this object and this direction. In section 40 of *BT* he tells us several times that the '*wovor*' of anxiety is '*the world as such*' (p. 231, Heidegger's italics) or '*being-in-the-world-itself*' (p. 232, Heidegger's italics). In the same section he writes that 'in anxiety what is environmentally ready-to-hand sinks away

1. Wolfgang Stegmüller, *Main Currents in Contemporary German, British, and American Philosophy*, trans. A. D. Blumberg (Dordrecht Holland, 1969), p. 179.

2. Ibid., p. 161.

3. Søren Kierkegaard, *Concluding Unscientific Postscript*, trans. D. F. Swenson (Princeton, NJ, 1941), pp. 182 ff.

4. Heidegger, 'Was ist Metaphysik?' reprinted in *Wegmarken*, pp. 8–9. There is an English translation of this piece in Werner Brock, ed., *Existence and Being*. All quotations from 'Was ist Metaphysik?' are given in my own translation.

and, so in general, do entities within-the-world.' When all these entities 'sink away,' 'the "world" can offer nothing more, and neither can the Dasein-with of others' (p. 232). Saying that we are anxious in the face of the world as such, he tells us, is equivalent to the statement that we are anxious of the Nothing (p. 232, G p. 187). I do not profess to understand all of this, but talk about 'the Nothing' as the '*wovor*' of anxiety becomes much clearer when Heidegger discusses anxiety in connection with death. In a passage which I quoted in a previous section (p. 354, G p. 306) Heidegger tells us that 'the impossibility of existence,' which death is seen to be, is 'die schlechthinnige Nichtigkeit des Daseins'—'the utter nothingness (nullity) of Dasein.' It is utter nothingness which Dasein must face in anxiety. 'In this state-of-mind, Dasein finds itself *face-to-face* with the Nothing of the possible impossibility of its existence' (p. 310, G p. 266). Again: 'The Nothing with which anxiety brings us face-to-face, unveils the nothingness by which Dasein, in its very *basis* is defined; and this basis itself is thrownness into death (p. 356, G p. 308, Heidegger's italics).[1]

The nature of this Nothing is further explored in the first of the lectures which make up *Introduction to Metaphysics* and in several later writings. The Nothing is not a being or an object (*Gegenstand*). Nevertheless it is in some important sense real, and the fact that science does not recognize it only shows the narrowness of science: 'It is perfectly true that one cannot talk or deliberate about the Nothing, as though it were a thing like the rain outside or the mountain or any object whatsoever. The Nothing remains in principle inaccessible to science. A person who really wants to talk about the Nothing must become unscientific.'[2]

---

1. It is clearly Heidegger's view that when we think about death authentically we experience anxiety. It is not clear whether he is committed to the converse—to the view that anxiety is always anxiety of death (*Todesangst*). This is not clear because of the obscurity of his various remarks that the '*wovor*' of anxiety is 'the world as such' and 'being-in-the-world-itself'. None of this is ever adequately explained, either by Heidegger or by any of his devotees. Otto Pöggeler, a leading Heidegger scholar, does not seem to be sure either. In one passage (*Der Denkweg Martin Heideggers* [Pfullingen, 1963], p. 301) he speaks of 'anxiety which is *essentially* anxiety of death' (my italics), leaving open the possibility that anxiety can also be experienced in situations in which we are not face-to-face with death.

2. Heidegger, *Einführung in die Metaphysik*, 2nd ed. (Tübingen: Niemeyer, 1958), pp. 19–20. An English translation of this book by Ralph Manheim was published by Yale University Press in 1959. Manheim's translation is a respectable job but seriously misleads the reader in translating Heidegger's '*das Nichts*' simply as 'nothing' without even capitalizing the word. English translations of Heidegger's books do not usually receive critical reviews by analytical philosophers. This volume is an exception. It was reviewed incisively and amusingly both by Walter Cerf in *Philosophy and Phenomenological Research* (1961): 109–12, and by Anthony Quinton in *Philosophical Books* (1960): 11–13.

It must be remembered that no 'strictness of a science reaches the seriousness of metaphysics' and that 'philosophy can never be judged by the standards of science.'[1] In fact, for reasons we shall not go into here, Heidegger maintains that science itself is possible only because man 'projects himself into the Nothing.'[2] In volume 2 of his *Nietzsche* Heidegger denounces with great vehemence the philosophers who make fun of his talk about the Nothing as an 'empty play with words.' The so-called 'reflections' of these people are impressive only as long as we 'move in the region of what is easily intelligible.' His opponents are guilty of gross 'thoughtlessness' and, in contrast to Heidegger himself, 'operate with mere words.' Although it is not easy to talk about it without appearing to involve oneself in contradiction, the Nothing is very real and 'need not be sought or found' if only because it is 'what we can never lose.'[3]

The Nothing is not only in some sense real, but it also engages in an activity or a quasi activity to which Heidegger refers as *nichten*, variously translated as 'nihilating' or 'nothinging'. The Nothing is 'essentially repulsing' (or 'repelling'—the German is 'wesenhaft abweisend'). This 'nothinging' or 'repulsing' is not the same thing as annihilation (*Vernichtung*); and it also is not identical with negation (*Verneinung*), although negation is not unrelated to the nothinging of the Nothing. Originally, the Nothing is present as a datum[4] only in anxiety, but much else 'testifies' to its 'constant although admittedly veiled presence.'[5] Negation as a logical operation 'is grounded in the Nothing, i.e., it originates from the nothinging of the Nothing.' In a passage which has frequently been quoted Heidegger asks, 'Is the Nothing real only because of the existence of the not, i.e., of negation? Or is it the other way around: do negation and

---

1. *W*, p. 18.

2. Ibid., pp. 17–18. The German original is, 'dieses wissenschaftliche Dasein ist nur möglich, wenn es sich im vorhinein in das Nichts hineinhält.'

3. *Nietzsche*, 2:51.

4. The word 'datum' is not Heidegger's but that of his follower, William Barrett (*Irrational Man*, p. 252). Barrett also refers to the Nothing as 'a strange negative entity' (ibid.). Heidegger himself would probably wish to avoid the word 'entity', but he would approve of the remainder of this description. The Nothing, as we found, is inaccessible to science or ordinary observation quite unlike 'the rain outside or the mountain or any object whatsoever.' Arne Naess, in an exceedingly sympathetic presentation, speaks of the Nothing as a 'phenomenon.' 'Insofar as the nothing is disclosed,' writes Naess, 'it is a "phenomenon" in the first of the senses of the word Heidegger has announced he will use in his text. In this sense a phenomenon is something which shows-itself-by-itself' (*Four Modern Philosophers* [Chicago, 1968], p. 225).

5. *W*, p. 14.

the not exist only because of the reality of the Nothing?'[1] In opposition to the 'dominant and unquestioned teaching of "logic"' Heidegger replies that 'the Nothing is more original than the not and negation.'[2] Negation is only one and 'by no means the leading' mode of conduct that is grounded in the nothinging of the Nothing.[3] There are various other situations in which Dasein is 'thoroughly shaken' (*durchschüttert*) by the nothinging of the Nothing: 'Deeper than . . . mere rational negation is the harshness of opposition and the pungency of loathing. More responsible [than mere rational negation] is the pain of failure and the mercilessness of a prohibition, more burdensome the bitterness of renunciation.'[4]

Heidegger's view that, in the course of anxiety in the face of death, we experience the Nothing is endorsed not only by out-and-out Heideggerians but also by many more independent existentialists. They all believe that in some sense the Nothing, or Non-Being, is real—in a sense in which this is not allowed by positivists and most ordinary people—and that our most obvious (although not our only) encounter with the Nothing occurs in the course of our thoughts and feelings about death. Thus, Tillich, who like Heidegger believes that we cannot account for the existence of negative judgments without postulating the reality of 'non-being' (his word corresponding to Heidegger's 'the Nothing'), also maintains that we directly experience this non-being in the course of two 'shocks.' One of these 'shocks' is experienced by 'those who are philosophers by nature' when they realize in their 'theoretic imagination' that, although there *are* things, there might have been nothing. The other shock of non-being is one that can also be experienced by 'a simple human being.' One experiences it in 'the practical experience of having to die.'[5] Similarly, Macquarrie, who concedes that philosophers like Carnap 'have some excellent sport in shooting down the kind of talk [about the Nothing] which we meet in Heidegger and others' and who presumably agrees that Heidegger is mistaken in regarding 'nothing', in its ordinary sense, as a name, insists that Heidegger is not talking nonsense. Heidegger is not talking nonsense because 'nothing', as it is used by him, does have

---

1. *W*, pp. 5–6.
2. Ibid.
3. Ibid., pp. 13–14.
4. Ibid., p. 14.
5. Paul Tillich, *My Search for Absolutes* (New York: Simon and Schuster, 1967), pp. 81–82.

'something like an empirical anchor.'[1] In the 'existential situation' with which Heidegger is concerned, talk about the Nothing 'not only makes sense but very good sense indeed.'[2] The 'existential situation' which gives content to Heidegger's use of 'nothing' is 'the mood of anxiety' which 'discloses' to us 'the possibility of ceasing to be.' '"Nothing" stands for the disclosure in our experience as existents of this possibility of ceasing to be.'[3] Again: 'Anxiety makes manifest the nullity . . . that enters into the very constitution of man's being. . . . Anxiety in the face of death . . . brings man to confront nothing.'[4]

There is a great deal in the various statements by Heidegger and the other writers I have quoted which is in one way or another open to question. Among many other things, I find Heidegger's strictures on the 'they' in connection with its alleged 'veiling' of the indefiniteness of death totally absurd. It is true that death is 'possible at any moment,' but, unless we have strong reason to expect its occurrence in the immediate or very near future, it is just elementary good sense to treat it as something that will happen 'sometime later' (which—contrary to Heidegger's assertion—is not making it definite) and to get on with whatever 'urgency' may be at hand. The moment we bring the Heidegger-Stegmüller talk about 'enduring death as an indeterminate possibility' down to earth, it is seen to be empty and grotesque posturing. If a surgeon is about to operate to restore a person's health, should he not proceed with this 'urgency' in order to endure the indefiniteness of his death? If a singer is about to give a recital, should he cancel it so that he can instead cultivate the anxiety with which Heidegger wants us to contemplate the uncertain 'when' of his death? Should a person who is not very old and who is in good health not set out on a major project like a scientific investigation or the composition of a symphony just because he *may* die at any moment? If none of these suggestions are implied in Heidegger's recommendation, just what *is* its content? Turning to Heidegger's talk about the Nothing, the first and perhaps most obvious criticism is that he seems quite unable to provide a proper statement of what is at issue between him and those whom he calls the defenders of logic. According to Heidegger's formulation both of the

---

1. *SCE*, p. 85.
2. Ibid., p. 83.
3. Ibid., p. 85.
4. Ibid., p. 82.

opposing positions accept the reality of the Nothing, and the only question is whether the Nothing is more 'original' than negation. The fact is, of course, that Heidegger's opponents do *not* allow the reality of his Nothing: they maintain that in order to give an adequate account of the nature of negative judgments, we do not need to introduce such a weird referent at all. Again, nobody with the slightest intellectual honesty can be satisfied that Heidegger has adequately explained what he means by *nichten*, the 'nothing' in which the Nothing is supposedly engaged. However, I do not intend to pursue these and other pertinent objections here. I will confine myself to a discussion of two of Heidegger's claims: (1) that to give an adequate account of human moods, especially as they relate to death, we must include anxiety (in his special sense) as well as fear and (2) that if one admits the reality of anxiety as a special mood, one is thereby committed to accepting the reality of his Nothing. I shall give reasons for accepting (1) and for rejecting (2). More specifically, I shall try to show that Heidegger calls attention to something of interest in distinguishing anxiety, at least as it relates to death, from other members of the fear family. His formulations are oracular and exceedingly cryptic, but a sympathetic reading will show that he has a substantive point which can be stated simply and clearly. I will also try to show that admission of the facts about anxiety to which Heidegger calls attention does not imply any of his claims about the reality of the Nothing. Since a great many confusions surround the entire subject of absences and nothingness, even in the writings of philosophers who have no connection with existentialism, I will also offer a few clarifying comments of a more general nature.

I will begin by pointing out that in a certain quite straightforward sense, absences are just as real as presences. Some years ago I entertained a distinguished acquaintance at an expensive restaurant. I intended to express my appreciation of many kindnesses he had shown me over a number of years. When the bill came, I discovered to my great embarrassment that I had no money in my pocket. The absence of money was just as much a fact as the presence of money is a fact on other occasions. If I look in the refrigerator for oranges and find no other fruit than an apple and some peaches, I thereby discover the absence of oranges. The absence of oranges is just as real, just as indisputable a fact as the presence of the apple and the peaches. Just like presences, absences can be frightening, embarrassing, tragic, and also delightful. The absence of the sight of a person who has become blind is a tragic absence. The absence of money can be highly embarrassing. The absence of a hated tyrant, whether he is a political leader or the chairman of a department or the foreman in a factory, is exhilarating. The presence of an illness can be depressing and upsetting. The absence of the same illness, after it has been cured, can be a source of delight.

My statement that absences are real must not be misconstrued as committing me to various metaphysical theories that some readers, especially existentialists, are liable to read into it. In the first place I am not asserting the existence or reality of 'nonthings', a weird species of entity exemplified by nonoranges, nonmoney, noncancer, etc. Admitting that there are true negative statements no more requires one to postulate such nonthings than admitting that there are true disjunctions requires one to postulate 'disjunctive entities'. A naturalist examining footprints may be in a position to assert quite correctly, 'These are the footprints of a tiger or a lion.' To account for the truth of this statement it is not necessary to introduce an animal or quasi animal called 'lion or tiger' in addition to tigers and lions. Similarly, the truth of the statement 'there are no oranges in the refrigerator' does not presuppose that there are entities called 'nonoranges'. In saying that absences are real I am not saying also that the absence of absent things is one of their characteristics. The absence of absent oranges is not a characteristic of oranges in the way sweetness or roundness may be characteristics of oranges. Finally, I am not saying that there are 'negative facts' except in the innocuous sense in which this is another way of saying that there are true negative statements. I am *not* saying that there are negative facts in a sense in which this is a metaphysical thesis that has been advocated by many philosophers, for example, by Bertrand Russell in his lectures on 'The Philosophy of Logical Atomism.'[1] My objection to this thesis is not primarily to its postulation of *negative* facts but to its postulation of *facts* as part of the 'furniture of the world.' There are things which have qualities and stand in certain relations to one another, and we make true or false statements about them; but there is no reason for adding a further kind of entity, called 'facts', positive or negative. There are sweet red apples in the refrigerator, but there

---

1. Bertrand Russell, 'The Philosophy of Logical Atomism,' *Monist* (1918–19), reprinted in Russell's *Logic and Knowledge* (London: G. Allen and Urwin, 1956).

is not a further entity called 'the fact that there are sweet red apples in the refrigerator'. The expression 'it is a fact that' is not of course meaningless, but it is just another way of asserting a given statement.[1]

The admission of the reality of absences in the sense explained in no way commits one to accepting Heidegger's various statements about the Nothing. This can be shown independently of deciding whether Heidegger is talking sense in this connection or what the sense of his statements is, if they have any. It can be shown as the result of his quite explicit declaration that the Nothing cannot be discovered by ordinary observation, that it is a reality which falls outside the domain of scientific observation. Quite clearly, absences are ascertained by the same ordinary observations as presences. No special 'existential mood' and no 'noncalculative' or 'essential' thinking of the kind that supposedly gets us beyond beings or things-within-the-world is required to verify such statements as 'there are no oranges in the refrigerator' or 'there is no money in my pocket' or 'Samuel Blau is not suffering from cancer'. Absences, if I may talk in this way, are one thing; Heidegger's Nothing, if it is real at all, is quite another. It will be helpful to introduce the terms 'natural' and 'nonnatural' to bring out this distinction. A 'natural' fact or phenomenon is one which can be described in terms of an 'empiricist language' as this has been defined by Hempel.[2] A 'nonnatural' fact or phenomenon, if there is any, could not be described in an empiricist language. Using this terminology, I can state my point by saying that absences are natural phenomena—the absence of oranges or money or cancer *can* be expressed in an empiricist language—while the Nothing is conceded to be a 'nonnatural' phenomenon or reality.

---

1. Readers interested in these questions will find informative and clarifying discussions in A. N. Prior's articles 'Negation' and 'Correspondence Theory of Truth' (*Encyclopedia of Philosophy*, 5:458–63 and 2:223–32) and in the writings of Frank Ramsey, the later Wittgenstein, and the later G. E. Moore, on which Prior's discussions are based. The dispute over the 'existence' of negative facts does involve the entirely intelligible question whether, in Prior's words, 'signs of negation are really indispensable—whether what we say when we use them cannot be also said without them, and that more directly—whether signs of negation are just convenient abbreviations for complex forms in which no such signs enter.' It should be emphasized that whatever the answer to this question turns out to be, it cannot affect what I pointed out in the text, namely, that there are true statements containing signs of negation. These statements will remain true even if it should turn out that they are translatable into statements containing no signs of negation.

2. See, for example, Carl Hempel, 'The Empiricist Criterion of Meaning,' section 3. This article is available in many places, most conveniently in *Logical Positivism*, ed. A. J. Ayer (New York, 1959).

I next wish to discuss nothingness in the sense of the absence of all things or what I shall call 'the total absence'. Such a discussion will shed some light on what Heidegger does and what he does not mean by his Nothing. I first wish to show that nothingness in the sense of the absence of all things is a perfectly intelligible notion. I can do this most easily by assuming, for the sake of this discussion, that all things are material and that physics has established a law which I shall call 'the principle of continuous reduction of mass-energy'. This principle, as the name suggests, asserts that the quantity of mass-energy is constantly diminishing. Let us further suppose that we know the exact amount of mass-energy existing at the present time. It being assumed that we know the rate of diminishing, we will then be able to predict the ever-smaller quantities existing at later times, and we will also be able to predict when the quantity will be zero. At that time nothing would exist; the statement 'nothing exists' would have become true; there would be a total absence of things. Of course, the principle of continuous reduction is not a true description of the actual universe, and we have no reason whatever to suppose that there ever was or ever will be nothing, i.e., a total absence; but the only point at issue at the moment is that such a state of affairs is logically conceivable.

This conclusion has been challenged by many philosophers. Two of its most prominent opponents in the twentieth century are Bergson and Sartre. Sartre's discussion is exceedingly obscure, and I will here only consider Bergson's two chief arguments. They are meant to show that the notion of a total absence is a 'pseudo-idea, a mere word.'[1] Bergson's first argument is based on the consideration that when we think of the nonexistence of an object we 'replace' it in our thought by another object. It is true that any particular object 'can be supposed annihilated.' Not realizing that the suppression of a thing consists in the substitution of another, we infer that it is possible to suppress in thought all objects simultaneously and thereby think of a total absence. This inference is fallacious: 'If thinking the absence of one thing is only possible by the

---

1. Henri Bergson, *Creative Evolution*, trans. A. Mitchell (New York: H. Holt, 1911), p. 308. All quotations in the text are from the Modern Library reprint of 1944. Sidney Hook, in his 'The Quest for "Being",' wholeheartedly endorses Bergson's 'striking analysis' and makes it the basis of an argument against Heidegger's Nothing (*Journal of Philosophy* [1953]: 711 ff.). For an illuminating discussion of Sartre's various pronouncements about nothingness, see A. Plantinga, 'An Existentialist's Ethics,' *Review of Metaphysics* (1958).

more or less explicit representation of the presence of some other thing, if, in short, annihilation signifies before anything else substitution, the idea of an "annihilation of everything" is as absurd as that of a square circle.'[1] Bergson argues in effect that the statement 'nothing exists' is not merely false but self-contradictory because we cannot visualize or, more generally, have an image of a total absence. In reply it should be observed that this argument confuses logical with psychological considerations. It may well be true that we cannot visualize or imagine a total absence, but this shows nothing whatsoever about the logical status of the statement that nothing exists. From the fact that I or anybody else cannot frame an image of the absence of both of two things, A and B, it does not follow that their simultaneous absence is logically inconceivable, i.e., that the statements 'A does not exist' and 'B does not exist' cannot be true at the same time. Let us suppose that the universe consists of just three things, A, B, and C. Let us furthermore assume that all human beings are so constituted that whenever they think of the absence of one of these three things, they cannot help thinking of the presence of one of the others. Surely it would not follow that the simultaneous absence of all three things is logically inconceivable, i.e., that the statements 'A does not exist', 'B does not exist', and 'C does not exist' cannot be true at the same time.

It may be objected that in the above illustration the universe consists not of three but of at least four objects—A, B, C, and the person thinking about them (we will assume that there is only one such person). The person thinking about A, B, and C, it would be said, has not been 'supressed'. This is in effect Bergson's second argument. 'From the fact that two relative absences are imaginable in turn,' he writes, 'we wrongly conclude that they are imaginable together.' This conclusion is absurd because we cannot imagine an absence 'without perceiving, at least confusedly, that we are imagining it, consequently that we are acting, that we are thinking, and therefore that something still subsists.'[2] The argument is very similar to one commonly employed to show that we cannot conceive of our own death. It is said that in any attempt to do so we are surreptitiously present as 'spectators' of our own annihilation. Bergson himself

---

1. Bergson, *Creative Evolution*, p. 308.
2. Ibid., p. 303. I have substituted 'absence' for the quaint word 'nought' used by Bergson's translator. The French is *le néant*.

uses this very illustration to support his case against the conceivability of a total absence: 'I can, no doubt, interrupt by thought the course of my inner life; I may suppose that I sleep without dreaming or that I have ceased to exist; but at the very instant when I make this supposition, I conceive myself, I imagine myself watching over my slumber or surviving my annihilation.'[1]

The fallacy of this argument consists in the confusion of the content of a thought with its occurrence in the life of a given person. It is true that I cannot think of anything without being alive, but this shows nothing whatsoever about the content of my thoughts. More specifically, it does not show that in a given case *what* I am thinking about is one of my thoughts. Let us suppose that on May 11, 2004, I am thinking about the speech which Winston Churchill made to the House of Commons in 1940 after the fall of France. In order to do this I must be alive on May 11, 2004, but *what* I think about is Churchill's speech in 1940 and not my thought about it in 2004. I can think of my own death as easily as of the death of other people. To do this I must be alive, but again what I think about is *my annihilation* and not *my thinking about* my annihilation.[2] Similarly, the fact that I must be alive in order to think about the absence of all things in no way requires me to think about my existence at the time the thought occurs. My existence at that time does indeed show that the statement 'nothing exists' is *false*. It does not show, what is the point at issue, that it is self-contradictory or that I am unable to comprehend what *would* make it true.[3]

---

1. Bergson, *Creative Evolution*, p. 307. Bergson's argument is quite similar to one employed by Berkeley to prove that the notion of unperceived objects is self-contradictory (*The Principles of Human Knowledge*, section 23): 'But say you, surely there is nothing easier than to imagine trees, for instance, in a park, or books existing in a closet, and nobody to perceive them. I answer, you may so, there is no difficulty in it: but what is all this, I beseech you, more than framing in your mind certain ideas which you call *books* and *trees*, and at the same time omitting to frame the idea of any one that may perceive them? *but do not you yourself perceive or think of them all the while?*' (Berkeley's italics). The answer to Berkeley is exactly the same as the one to Bergson given in the text.

2. For a detailed discussion of the confusions of philosophers and others who believe that one's own death is inconceivable, see my article '"My Death"', *Encyclopedia of Philosophy* (New York, 1967), 5:461 ff.

3. The remarks in the text are sufficient to answer Bergson, but they require one significant qualification. The logical status of 'nothing exists now' is different in one interesting respect from that of the statements 'nothing will exist in the future' and 'nothing existed at some time in the past'. The latter two statements are not necessarily false, but the statement 'nothing exists now', uttered while the author of the statement exists, although not self-contradictory, is in a sense necessarily false. In this respect it is analogous to the statement 'I do not exist'. Both are instances of what some writers have called 'pragmatic contradictions'. I am grateful to Donald Levy for calling my attention to this point.

Is Heidegger's Nothing identical with the total absence just discussed? Heidegger himself has repeatedly disavowed such an identification and, what is more important, his most characteristic pronouncements preclude it. However, he does not have a single consistent position on the subject. Although much of what Heidegger says about anxiety, death, and specifically about the Nothing clearly implies that it must be distinguished from the total absence, there are some passages in his earlier writings of which we could not make any sense unless the Nothing is *there* understood as the absence of all things. Thus, at the opening of *An Introduction to Metaphysics* he raises the question, asked before him, among many others, by Leibniz, Voltaire, Schelling, and Scheler—'Why are there any things at all and not rather Nothing?' He insists that this is a question which no human being can totally avoid, remarking that 'each of us is grazed at least once, perhaps more than once, by the hidden power of this question.'[1] It must be emphasized, because of what Heidegger wrote in subsequent years, that in the question by whose power each of us has been 'grazed,' 'nothing' means 'not anything', so that the whole question comes to, 'Why are there things and not a total absence of things?' It should also be observed that although he capitalizes 'Nothing' he does not here, as he does on most other occasions, speak of '*the* Nothing'. In later, retrospective musings Heidegger insists that his question is not identical with the one discussed by Leibniz and Schelling: they were, and he was not, looking for 'the highest ground and the first cause of all beings which was itself treated as a being.'[2] It is true that Heidegger was not satisfied (and probably not looking for) the kind of answer arrived at by Leibniz and Schelling, but this does not show that he was not asking the same question. In any event he now (1955) tells us that he was really concerned with the question 'Why do people everywhere give priority to beings and do not rather think about the not of beings, this "Nothing," i.e., Being in its essence?' (ibid.). In what was probably Heidegger's last discussion of this issue—in a television interview in celebration of his eightieth birthday—he told the interviewer that for him 'the question has a totally different sense' from the one it has for Leibniz, Schelling, and other metaphysicians. He then explained that *his* question meant 'Why are beings given priority, why is the Nothing not thought of as

---

1. *IM*, p. 1.
2. 'Zur Seinsfrage,' *W*, p. 248.

identical with Being?' This last question, he goes on, amounts to asking, 'Why is the world dominated by forgetfulness of Being and where does this forgetfulness originate?'[1] Even if one grants that these last questions— about the essence of Being, the identity of Being, and the Nothing and the forgetfulness of Being—have some content, it is surely a very strange use of language to ask them by using the words 'Why are there things and not rather Nothing?' Moreover, the questions which Heidegger claims to have been concerned with are surely not the questions which everybody asks sooner or later and by whose power all of us have been grazed.

There can nevertheless be no doubt that most of the time and certainly in all the passages which are relevant to anxiety and human attitudes in the face of death, Heidegger's Nothing is not identical with the total absence. He himself is quite explicit about this in his later writings. In the Postscript to 'What Is Metaphysics?' (1943) he writes, 'We are guilty of a "cheap explanation" if we regard the Nothing as "merely negative" ["*das bloss Nichtige*"] and devoid of characteristics.'[2] Again, in a lecture given in 1938 and reprinted in *Holzwege*, he observes that 'the Nothing is never nothing just as little as it is something in the sense of being an object.'[3] In 'Zur Seinsfrage', he explains that the Nothing, just like Being, cannot be said to exist but is nevertheless real. He tries to convey this by saying that neither Being nor Nothing *ist* ('is'), but that 'it gives' both of them. This sounds less peculiar in German, since *es gibt* is a common equivalent for 'there is'.[4] This

1. Quoted in Karl Rahner, *Martin Heidegger im Gespräch*, ed. R. Wisser (Freiburg and Munich: K. Alber, 1970), p. 75.

2. *W*, p. 102.

3. Heidegger, *Holzwege* (Frankfurt, 1950), p. 104.

4. In most of his later writings, when Heidegger wishes to speak of the kind of reality possessed by Being, the Nothing, or the 'Fourfold', he uses *wesen*, a verb he coined specially for this purpose. Sentences like 'Das Sein west' or 'Das Nichts west' are common throughout Heidegger's later works. There is a German noun *Wesen* which means 'essence', but Heidegger derives his verb from the German word *Anwesenheit*, which means 'presence'. Heidegger repeatedly speaks of the 'Anwesenheit des anwesenden' (The presence of the Present). Some of his more unrestrained American disciples have followed Heidegger's example and coined the verb 'to presence'. Their translations of Heidegger as well as their own writings abound with the sentence 'the Presence presences'. Heidegger attributes the insight that 'the Presence presences' to the pre-Socratics. He merely claims to have rediscovered it. Unfortunately, explanations of what this pronouncement means are not provided. Both here and elsewhere Heidegger and his followers appear to operate on the principle that, if it is repeated often enough, even the most nebulous locution will become familiar and *seem* to be intelligible. It is well to recall a comment made by Cardinal Newman: 'Nothing is more common than for men to think that because they are familiar with words, they understand the ideas they stand for.'

Nothing 'which is not a being . . . is nevertheless nothing negative,' and Heidegger angrily defends 'What Is Metaphysics?' against the charge of 'nihilism,' insisting that 'the mentioned Nothing is not the Nothing in the sense of the negative Nothing.'[1] However, aside from these declarations, there are at least three reasons for not interpreting Heidegger's Nothing as the absence of all things. In the first place, and most obviously, Heidegger believes that '"it gives" Nothing,' i.e., that the Nothing is real *right now* when there are plenty of things. The existence of things implies that the statement 'nothing exists' is false in the sense in which it is about the absence of all things; but the existence of things is apparently quite compatible with the reality of Heidegger's Nothing. Secondly, Heidegger's Nothing, as we saw, is a highly active reality. Some passages in *An Introduction to Metaphysics*, in fact, read like a Manichean tract: two deities, a beneficent one called 'Being' and a malevolent one called the 'Nothing', are battling it out. The former tries to keep things in existence in opposition to the attempts of the latter to destroy them. Again, in volume 2 of *Nietzsche*, a book composed in the 1930s, he writes, 'Being means that beings are and that they are not absent. Being refers to this "that" as the decisiveness of the insurrection against the Nothing.'[2] All such passages about the activities of the Nothing imply that it is not identical with the total absence of things, since the latter could not possibly be active. Finally, the total absence can be described in an empiricist language. It is after all just a conjunction of the absence of pears, the absence of money, the absence of elephants, etc. In the imaginary universe governed by the principle of continuous reduction of mass-energy, we could predict when the last unit of mass-energy will disappear. The prediction that at a certain time the quantity of mass-energy will be zero would not only be based on just the kind of evidence on which scientific statements are generally founded, but it would also employ only the empirical and logical terms which make up the statements of an empiricist language. Heidegger's Nothing, on the other hand, according to his own declara-

1. *W*, p. 247.
2. *Nietzsche*, 2:399.

tion, is not the kind of reality which can even in principle be described in an empiricist language.[1]

It is time to return to anxiety and death. I remarked a little earlier that, in his insistence that anxiety (in his special sense) is the mood which corresponds to death, Heidegger calls attention to some interesting facts. I will now try to explain in my own words what these facts are. The fear of death, understood as the fear of *deadness*, is a unique fear. All or at least all the most familiar fears are in one way or another concerned with pain and suffering. We are afraid of 'detrimental' objects, to use Heidegger's word, because they are liable to kill us or because they are going to hurt us. We are afraid of objects, but we are also afraid of painful experiences. Deadness, however, is not a painful experience. It is not an experience at all. When I am dead, I will not be in pain, I will not be ill, I will not be rejected, unfairly criticized, or in any other way mistreated. However, even after I have realized this, the prospect of deadness continues to be horrifying and at times quite unbearable. In a letter, written not long before his own death, Einstein alluded to the same facts. 'Approached rationally,' he wrote, 'that fear [the fear of death] is the most unjustified of all fears, for there is no risk of any accidents to one who is dead.' The fear of death is therefore 'stupid,' but even so it 'cannot be helped.'[2]

I am not sure that the words 'fear' or 'anxiety' or any other term taken from the fear family are appropriate names for the mood that comes over

---

1. I believe that this account fairly reproduces the dominant trend in Heidegger's views about the Nothing. However, for the sake of completeness, it must be mentioned that in his later writings, as some passages quoted earlier indicated, he frequently identifies the Nothing with Being. Thus, in the passage in *Holzwege* which I quoted in the text and in which Heidegger assures us that 'the Nothing is never nothing,' he proceeds to assert that it 'is Being itself.' Similarly, in the preface to the third edition of *Vom Wesen des Grundes* (1949) he writes, 'The Nothing is the Not of beings and thus is Being experienced from the point of view of beings' (*W*, p. 21). In the Postscript to 'What Is Metaphysics?' he is equally definite: 'The Nothing . . . unveils itself as that which is distinct from all beings, to which we refer as "Being"' (*W*, p. 106). Finally, in 'Zur Seinsfrage,' in his retrospective discussion of what he supposedly did in 'What Is Metaphysics?' Heidegger tells us that 'since the question "what is metaphysics?" thinks right from the start only . . . the *transcendens*, the Being of beings, it can reach the Not of beings, *that* Nothing which is . . . identical with Being.' (*W*, p. 249). Heidegger evidently identifies the Nothing with Being on the ground that both are 'other than' or distinct from beings. This is a highly dubious reason, for even if one grants that there are realities which transcend beings, it is not at all obvious that they must all be one and the same. The identification of the Nothing with Being is also completely inconsistent with the Manichean passages found in the writings of the 1930s, which seem to express an essential feature of Heidegger's 'ontology.'

2. Quoted in Banesch Hoffman, *Albert Einstein, Creator and Rebel* (New York: Viking Press, 1972), p. 261.

thoughtful people when they fully realize the finality of death. Whatever
the label we decide on, I cannot agree that the mood is 'stupid.' It is true
that when I am dead I will not suffer. It would also be conceded by most
people that an infinite period of deadness is greatly preferable to a life of
infinite duration which is filled with excruciating pain. At the same time
it is difficult to bear the thought that, after I have died, I will be unable—
for all eternity—to do any of the things which made life interesting and
enjoyable and, what is equally unfortunate, to do any of the things I
would have liked to do but never did. The sting here comes from the *eternity* of the period of nonexistence after death. Death is unlike sleep not
only in that it involves the absence of any consciousness, but also in that
no return to consciousness is possible. If one were in a state of unconsciousness a few thousand or even a few million years, but if one were
assured of a return for, say, another seventy years and if this were followed by further such cycles, the prospect of enormously long periods of
total unconsciousness would not be unbearable and might on the contrary
be rather pleasing. It is not just the totality of the absence but the eternity
of this totality which most people find so unbearable. From Lucretius on,
philosophers have tried to lessen people's concern about death by
pointing out that we also did not exist for an infinite period before we
were born; and yet we do not feel any similar fear or concern about that
nonexistence. Unfortunately, these reflections do not usually have a
soothing effect.

   In the absence of any better suggestion I will continue to use Heidegger's word 'anxiety' to refer to the mood we have been discussing. We
have seen that anxiety in this sense is a mood which *in a sense* does not
have an object. I am afraid (or horrified) without being afraid of anything
unpleasant that may happen to me, of any painful experiences. I am afraid
without being afraid of *any* experiences. This is Heidegger's point and it
is a sound observation, but it in no way requires us to subscribe to the
reality of his Nothing. A little reflection shows that deadness is another
absence. It is true that my deadness, my annihilation, is not an absence I
can observe the way I can observe the absence of oranges in the refrigerator or the absence of money in my pocket, but neither could I observe
my nonexistence before birth. When deadness horrifies me I am concerned about the absence for all eternity of any further experiences that
would be *my* experiences, the experiences of Paul Edwards. This absence,

like the absence of oranges or the absence of money, can be fully described in the terms of an empiricist language. Using the terminology introduced earlier, it is a 'natural' reality. Heidegger's Nothing, on the other hand, by his own stipulation, is a nonnatural reality. If we call my nonexistence after death, or for that matter my nonexistence before birth, 'my nothingness', we can say that my nothingness is not Heidegger's Nothing. Even if there is such a reality as his Nothing, it is *not* what we are 'face-to-face with' in our anxiety about death.

Five

Double-Talk about Life after Death

B ertrand Russell makes Heidegger's point about the totality of the destruction which death involves not only more simply and clearly but also without any equivocation on the subject of survival. The reader will be surprised to hear that, in spite of his completely unqualified assertion that death is 'the impossibility of every way of comporting one-self towards anything, of every way of existing' and his equally unquali-fied characterization of death as a total nullity, Heidegger also claims that his analysis leaves the question of survival entirely open. His 'this-worldly ontological interpretation of death,' we are told, 'takes prece-dence over any ontical other-worldly speculation,' but he does not at all rule out such speculation. His investigation 'does not imply any ontical decision whether "after death" still another Being is possible, either higher or lower, or whether Dasein "lives on" or even "outlasts" itself and is "immortal."￼ Nor is anything decided ontically about the "other-worldly" and its possibility, any more than about the "this-worldly" (p. 292).[1] Heidegger's followers seem entirely satisfied that there is no incompatibility between these two sets of statements. 'Heidegger's onto-logical analysis,' writes Schrag approvingly, 'remains intentionally neu-

---

1. In 'Der Feldweg' (a little essay published in 1953) Heidegger writes that 'knowing joy is a door to the eternal' (Frankfurt, 1953), p. 6. We are not told whether this is to be construed as an 'ontic' decision in favor of survival.

tral to the material content of any special ontic interpretation of death. He has sought to clarify the ontological-existentialist foundation which is presupposed by any ontic-existential understanding, but he has not taken into his program the task of elucidating death in connection with its biological, psychological, or theological significance.'[1] 'The question,' furthermore, 'of man having some kind of 'being' after death is left open. . . . Heidegger's interpretation of man, as ontology, remains indifferent to any material content which may be supplied by a religious world-view or theological conviction.'[2] In much the same way Alwin Diemer maintains that Heidegger's conclusions about death do not 'in the least' amount to a 'denial of the immortality of men.' Those who attribute such a position to Heidegger 'confuse ontological and ontic problems.'[3] Unlike Heidegger, Schrag proceeds to inform us how the ontic question of survival *is* to be resolved. 'There,' he writes, 'man's concrete ethical and religious experience must constitute the court of final appeal.'[4] Schrag in one place discusses suicide and I believe he would claim his conclusion to be entirely consistent with Heidegger's teachings about death. Suicide, he tells us, 'provides no exit—neither the suicide in which the self succumbs to weakness nor the suicide of a defiant self-affirmation. Suicide solves only the problem of bodily annihilation, but the self is not exhausted in its mode as a living body.'[5]

I confess I find all of this extremely puzzling. If death is really 'the impossibility of *every* way of comporting oneself towards anything and of *every* way of existing,' if it is an utter nullity, then we do not survive. Conversely, if the question of survival is left open, then we have no right to declare, flatly, as something true without qualification, that death is an utter nullity. I do not know of anything that could be plainer than this. The statement that 'ontologically' death is indeed total annihilation, but that 'ontically' we may nevertheless survive, shows only one thing, namely that much of the time the distinction between 'ontological' and 'ontic' questions is exceedingly nebulous. One is reminded of the medieval doctrine of the 'twofold truth,' according to which a proposi-

---

1. *EF*, p. 117.
2. Ibid., p. 118.
3. Alwin Diemer, 'Grundzüge Heideggerschen Philosophierens,' *Zeitschrift für Philosophische Forschung* (1950–51): 562.
4. *EF*, p. 118.
5. Ibid., p. 110.

tion may be false as a matter of reason but nevertheless true as a matter of faith. If 'ontologically' death is total annihilation, this is presumably a true statement; and if it is a true statement, in what sense could it also not be true? Moreover, all of Heidegger's talk about anxiety (as contrasted with fear), as well as his numerous comments about the flight from this anxiety on the part of everyday Dasein, makes no sense unless death is really total annihilation.

Although the distinction between 'ontological' and 'ontic' is never clearly explained, either by Heidegger or by any of his followers, one does in *certain contexts* get a reasonably good idea of what is intended. An 'ontological' characteristic of human beings appears to be one which is essentially connected with their humanity; an 'ontic' characteristic is one that is not so connected. My concern for the future, my 'running ahead' of myself, for example, would be an ontological characteristic because it is essentially connected with my humanity; and the same would apply to the fact that I can and must make choices. The fact that I weigh 150 pounds or that I like steak but don't like fish are ontic characteristics, since I would or could be a human being even if my weight and tastes were different. The same is true of *specific* choices I make. That I can and must make choices is an ontological feature, but that I choose this rather than that is an ontic fact. Heideggerians usually explain the distinction by saying that ontological discourse is connected with Being, while ontic statements refer to things or beings. Ontology for Heidegger, in the words of Herbert Spiegelberg, one of the most reliable and sober expositors of the theories of phenomenologists and existentialists, is 'the study of Being as opposed to that of the things-in-being.'[1] 'Ontological inquiry,' Heidegger himself writes, 'is more primordial, as over against the ontical inquiry of the positive sciences' (*BT*, p. 31). Macquarrie and Robinson, in a footnote, point out that Heidegger does not explicitly define the words 'ontological' and 'ontical', but they add that 'their meanings will emerge rather clearly.' They then add their own explanations: 'Ontological inquiry is concerned primarily with *Being*; ontical inquiry is concerned primarily with entities and the facts about them' (M-R's italics). 'For Heidegger,' writes Webster F. Hood, 'to conceive something in its ontic dimension means that one grasps how it is related to other enti-

---

1. Herbert Spiegelberg, *The Phenomenological Movement*, 2nd ed. (The Hague, 1965), 2:290.

ties; but to conceive something in its ontological dimension is to appreciate how it is related to Being, to appreciate exactly how Being makes this entity possible.'[1] Father Demske, who defines ontology as 'the science of being,' explains that 'ontological' refers to 'the deeper level of intelligibility, the realm of the underlying structures,' while 'ontic' refers to 'the more immediate surface level of the concrete acts of existence.' 'Ontological', again, refers to 'the internal structures which underlie and constitute the being of a being as its conditions of possibility.' 'Ontic', on the other hand, refers to 'those actions which are externally observable, which are made possible by ontological structures.'[2] Since the word 'Being' is notoriously obscure, these definitions are not very helpful. William Barrett speaks of Being as 'the unutterable,'[3] and Heidegger himself has spoken of it as the 'das Ungreifbare' (the ungraspable), 'das Unbestimmte, Unbestimmbare' (that which cannot be specified, the indefinable), 'das Unumgängliche' (that which cannot be covered or surrounded), and 'das sich verbergende Einzige' (the unique that conceals itself).[4] Richard Schmitt, a critical and very able commentator, argues that 'the distinction between ontic and ontological talk closely parallels the familiar distinction that is often referred to by contrasting factual statements with statements about categories,' admitting that the latter is not itself a clear distinction.[5] I do not see that any of these interpretations, even allowing them to be coherent, avoid the inconsistency I have mentioned. Confining myself to Father Demske's formulation, it seems quite absurd to maintain *both* that on the 'deeper level of intelligibility' death amounts to total annihilation *and* that on 'the more immediate surface level of life' which is 'externally observable' human beings may nevertheless live forever.

Schrag's statement that 'suicide provides no exit' is equally inconsistent with Heidegger's 'ontological' analysis. The late Percy Bridgman was not only a distinguished physicist but also a man of great courage and integrity. When he found that he was suffering from incurable cancer he shot himself. If Heidegger is right in regarding death as total annihilation,

1. Webster F. Hood, 'The Aristotelian versus the Heideggerian Approach to the Problem of Technology,' in *Philosophy and Technology*, ed. C. Mitcham and R. Mackey (New York, 1972), p. 253.
2. *BMD*, p. 17.
3. Barrett, *Irrational Man*, p. 210.
4. *Vom Wesen der Wahrheit* (Frankfurt, 1943), pp. 19, 23, and 25.
5. Richard Schmitt, *Martin Heidegger on Being Human* (New York, 1969), p. 17.

then Professor Bridgman's suicide *did* provide an exit—he saved himself from what he regarded as pointless misery and pain. The self may not be 'exhausted in its mode as a living body,' but if death is 'the impossibility of *every* way of existing,' then any of the self's modes other than 'its mode as a living body' would also be annihilated. As for Schrag's claim that 'ethical and religious experience constitute the court of final appeal' in settling such questions as that of survival, it should be remarked that it involves a confusion between causal or genetic questions and questions of justification. Powerful religious experiences or ethical demands may *cause* a man to believe in survival. This does not mean that they *justify* such a belief, i.e., that they are any kind of evidence for it. It is far from clear, for example, how ethical or religious experiences could cancel out the overwhelming evidence we have that human consciousness is causally dependent on the brain and nervous system.[1]

Glenn Gray first refers to the 'existential dread' which grips us when we contemplate 'the prospect of no longer being, of vanishing into nullity.'[2] 'The positivist,' we are assured in this connection, 'has no weapon against this dread, this shudder at Non-being.'[3] The Heideggerian, it appears, who has achieved 'genuine personality' and therefore 'resoluteness,' does have a weapon. 'He will no longer avoid exposure nor the shudder of dread before Nothingness. On the contrary these will be his meat and drink.'[4] Whatever one may think of these 'weapons,' it seems clear that the 'authentic' individual who has achieved 'genuine personality' will truthfully regard death as a 'nullity,' i.e., as total annihilation. When we get to the end of the same essay, however, we find that the genuine personality is nevertheless entitled to faith in a hereafter. We are told that 'there must be some deep-seated faith that we are not suspended over an abyss.' Although we may have a yearning for rationality, this yearning 'must make place for religious faith and larger meanings.' We 'need not renounce our conviction that death as an occurrence holds, also, the promise of a greater fullness of Being.'[5] I should perhaps add that I am

---

1. For a detailed discussion of the confusion between genetic and logical questions on the part of religious existentialists see my Lindley Lecture, *Buber and Buberism—A Critical Evaluation* (Lawrence: University of Kansas Press, 1970), pp. 44f.

2. PD, pp. 55–56.

3. Ibid.

4. Ibid., p. 62.

5. Ibid., p. 67.

endlessly astonished that many Christians, Catholics as well as Protestants, are followers of Heidegger and have expressed their *total* acceptance of his teachings on death. They appear to see no inconsistency in accepting Heidegger's view that death is a 'total nullity' and their Christian faith in eternal life after death. Thus John Macquarrie, who is a leading Protestant theologian, in the very same book in which he defends Heidegger's views on death,[1] also has extensive discussions of eschatology in an entirely affirmative spirit, implying that Christian statements about the eternal life awaiting us after death are perfectly correct. I hope that one of these days a Christian follower of Heidegger will explain how it is possible to maintain *both* that death means total annihilation *and* that in spite of this total annihilation we shall live forever.[2]

---

1. *SCE.*

2. Lest the remarks in the text be misunderstood, I hasten to add that many Catholic and Protestant philosophers are anything but supporters of Heidegger's ideas. Anthony Kenny, an Oxford philosopher of great ability with a Catholic background, has repeatedly expressed his contempt both for Heidegger himself and for various of his followers. Thus, in a review of Paul Ricoeur's contribution to a book entitled *The Religious Significance of Atheism*, Kenny writes, 'Ricoeur's discussion is shored up, at crucial points, by gaseous quotations from Heidegger in which the obvious is reiterated with bombinating opacity' ('The Listener,' February 5, 1970). Father Copleston, whose standing as a philosopher and a historian of philosophy compares more than favorably with that of such Heideggerian clerics as Fathers Richardson, Demske, and Boros, treated Heidegger with disdain in vol. 7 of his monumental *History of Philosophy* (London, 1963), pp. 437f.

Acknowledgments

Some materials in the present book have appeared previously. I want to thank the editors of *Mind*, *Philosophy*, and *The Monist* for permission to reprint them here. The article in *The Monist* on Heidegger and death was subsequently expanded into a *Monist Monograph* published in 1979.

I want to thank Jonathan Glover, Donald Levy, Terence Penelhum, J. J. C. Smart, and Michael Wreen for reading the manuscript and making helpful suggestions. Professor Norbert Hoerster has kindly kept me informed of developments in Germany and France. Although German is my native language and I had little difficulty translating Heidegger himself even when this meant translating meaningless German into meaningless English, Gadamer's lyrical effusions were too much for me. The late Stefan Bauer-Mengelberg came to the rescue and translated the passages from Gadamer into appropriately lyrical English.

Index